MAYAS, AZTECS, AND INCAS

Mysteries of Ancient Civilizations

MAYAS, AZTECS, AND INCAS:

Mysteries of Ancient Civilizations of Central and South America

Mark J. Dworkin

Canadian Cataloguing in Publication Data

Dworkin, Mark J.
Mayas Aztecs and Incas

Includes bibliographical references.
ISBN 0-7710-2967-5

1. Mayas.   2. Aztecs.   3. Incas.   I. Title.

E65.D8 1990   970.004'97   C89-095346-5

Photos research: Jane Affleck
Maps by: James B. Loates

Printed and bound in Canada by
T. H. Best Printing Company Limited

McClelland & Stewart Inc.
The Canadian Publishers
481 University Avenue
Toronto, Ontario
M5G 2E9

Mayas, Aztecs, and Incas

Mysteries of the Ancient Civilizations of
Mexico
Central America
and
South America

THE MAYAS — builders of a great civilization with many more pyramids than ancient Egypt, and developers of an advanced mathematical system, yet they did this without metal, the wheel, or beasts of burden

THE AZTECS — followers of a religion that demanded a constant supply of human blood for its gods, they built a city rivalling any other in the world, only to be defeated and destroyed by a small number of Spanish invaders in league with local Amerindians previously subject to Aztec rule

THE INCAS — conquerors and unifiers of a great empire comparable in size with that of Alexander the Great, with a genius for engineering and organization, they overcame incredible geographic barriers in the Andes Mountains, yet their empire fell apart quickly following the invasion of the Spaniards

With a complete and up-to-date bibliography of books and articles for further reading and student research

ACKNOWLEDGEMENTS

I am very indebted to Tilly Crawley for suggesting and patiently editing this book. I owe an enormous debt of gratitude to Dr. Andrew Forester of the University of Toronto, an inveterate Mayanist whose deep love for his subject stimulates everyone who comes into contact with him. Frequent and long conversations with him have helped to clarify many points dealt with in the text of this book, leading me to correct errors and sins of omission, and to redirect emphases more properly.

I would also like to express my appreciation to Sue Jeffries of the Gardiner Museum and Marilyn Jenkins of the Royal Ontario Museum for allowing me access to their files on the civilizations described in the pages that follow. In addition, I should like to acknowledge those authors, historians, and archaeologists whose works have both fascinated me and provided me with valuable insights for this book: C. A. Burland, Michael D. Coe, John Crow, Charles Gallenkamp, Victor W. von Hagen, John Hemming, John S. Henderson, Hubert Herring, Mark Littman, Loren McIntyre, Tatiana Proskouriakoff, Linda Schele, Jacques Soustelle, Gene S. Stuart, and Wilson G. Turner.

The attempt to be comprehensive within a limited space has led me to be selective, and others may correctly dispute my choices and emphases. Naturally I am responsible for all interpretations and opinions, and for any errors that may unfortunately still remain.

Mark Dworkin
Head of History, Sir Sandford Fleming Secondary School

NOTE TO THE READER

Pre-Columbian civilizations have long been treated only briefly, if at all, at the senior secondary school level. This is a most unfortunate situation considering both the intrinsic fascination of these civilizations and the many things these ancient peoples have to teach us about themselves, ourselves, and about life.

Although the study of ancient civilizations opens a door on the fascinating world of the past, these civilizations may at first glance seem to be remote from our modern world. But they have influenced our lives in a number of ways. For example, pre-Columbian Amerindian visual art forms are seen everywhere today . Many of the things we eat, such as corn, potatoes, tomatoes, pumpkins, peppers, squash, beans, and even chocolate, were introduced by these prehistoric peoples. Even some of our words, like tomato, chocolate, chili, and coyote are of Amerindian origin. As well, the emerging and increasingly important nations of Central and South America, such as Mexico and Peru, owe much of their heritage to their pre-Columbian past.

This book attempts to survey the great civilizations of South and Central America before Columbus, and their reactions to the arrival of the Europeans, providing students with an introduction to the great variety of cultures from this ancient period. It paints a picture of the chronological development of pre-Columbian Mexican, Central American, and South American civilizations, beginning with the first crossings of the Bering Straits at least 10 000 years ago, and ending with the Spanish arrival five centuries ago. The survey covers the important aspects of the culture of each civilization. While many questions are raised, few are definitively answered, as archaeologists are constantly making new discoveries, which necessitate a rethinking of earlier ideas. Future excavations and more advanced methods of analyzing finds will answer many of these questions, and at the same time undoubtedly make some of the few certainties advanced here obsolete. This is the destiny of any book on this subject.

The chapters of this book are self-contained and may be read in any sequence. The first chapter helps to provide a background for the following three, but it too may also be read by itself. Each section contains an extensive bibliography of books and journal articles for the student who wishes to read and research further.

A note on usage: the text uses the more modern B.C.E. and C.E. for *Before the Common Era* and *Common Era* in place of B.C. and A.D.

Above all this book is meant to open up for the student the marvellous and puzzling world of the ancient American civilizations.

TABLE OF CONTENTS

CHAPTER ONE: THE FIRST AMERICANS

CHAPTER TWO: THE MAYA

CHAPTER THREE: THE AZTECS

THE FIRST AMERICANS

In prehistoric times Asian hunters migrated across the Bering Straits, adapted to a variety of environments, and eventually built the first civilizations in the western hemisphere.

INTRODUCTION

The Spanish voyagers who crossed the ocean in 1492 with Christopher Columbus, and those who followed in subsequent decades, took part in what was possibly the most shocking series of meetings between civilizations in all of history. To the complete and total surprise of the Europeans, there existed in the "New World" two highly advanced and sophisticated civilizations — the Aztec and the Inca empires.

> "... when we saw all those cities and villages built in the water, and other great towns on dry land, and that straight and level causeway leading to Mexico, we were astounded. These great towns and pyramids and buildings rising from the water, all made of stone, seemed like an enchanted vision ... a dream ... " Bernal Diaz del Castillo, *The Discovery and Conquest of Mexico, 1517-1521.*

Immediately, speculation began in Europe about the origins of these peoples. Europeans interested in the study of ancient times, called *antiquarians*, believed the people the Spaniards called "red men" (because of the red paint they wore on their faces) must surely have had some previous contact with European or Asian peoples, contact long since forgotten by history.

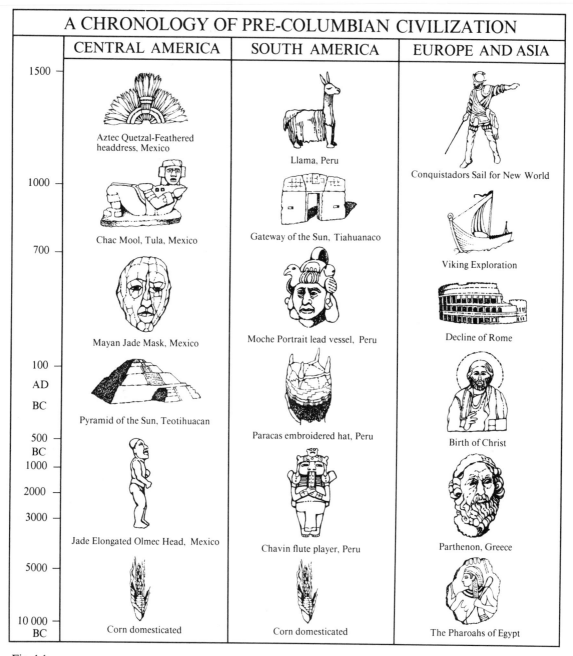

A CHRONOLOGY OF PRE-COLUMBIAN CIVILIZATION

	CENTRAL AMERICA	SOUTH AMERICA	EUROPE AND ASIA
1500	Aztec Quetzal-Feathered headdress, Mexico	Llama, Peru	Conquistadors Sail for New World
1000	Chac Mool, Tula, Mexico	Gateway of the Sun, Tiahuanaco	Viking Exploration
700	Mayan Jade Mask, Mexico	Moche Portrait lead vessel, Peru	Decline of Rome
100 AD BC	Pyramid of the Sun, Teotihuacan	Paracas embroidered hat, Peru	Birth of Christ
500 BC 1000 2000 3000	Jade Elongated Olmec Head, Mexico	Chavin flute player, Peru	Parthenon, Greece
5000			
10 000 BC	Corn domesticated	Corn domesticated	The Pharoahs of Egypt

Fig. 1.1

This chart allows you to compare the approximate dates at which civilizations in Central America, South America, and Europe and Asia developed.

The Spaniards shared the **ethnocentric** world view of all Europeans at that time: that white European Christians were the most civilized and advanced of all people on earth. All other peoples were inherently inferior, so the Europeans thought. It was inconceivable to them that a non-white, non-European people could have become so advanced on their own.

Yet centuries before Christopher Columbus first set sail across the ocean in 1492, there existed on the American continents hundreds of different Amerindian nations. While some of these nations had very simple cultures, others had developed remarkable urban civilizations, perhaps more advanced than any in Europe or Asia at a corresponding time. The most notable of these civilizations were centered in three widely separated regions: in the central valley of Mexico, in Central America, and in the Andes Mountains of South America. This period of history, before the arrival of Columbus, is often referred to by scholars as the **pre-Columbian** period of history.

By the time the Spanish arrived in Central America at the end of the fifteenth century, many of these civilizations were already long dead, their urban centres abandoned and overgrown with vegetation. Their beautiful buildings had crumbled, their woodwork had rotted, and their cultural achievements were largely forgotten. The **Aztec** and **Inca** nations that the Spanish encountered had built upon the ruins of these earlier peoples, in some cases on the very foundations of buildings that had belonged to people long-disappeared or absorbed into the Aztec and Inca empires.

Who were these people who had built such remarkable civilizations before they disappeared, and where had they come from?

BERINGIA

Archaeologists think that the **precursors** of the people who were to build these great civilizations in South and Central America came from central Asia, via Siberia, about 12 000 to 40 000 years ago; some experts claim that they came as long as 70 000 years ago. These first migrants came across a narrow land bridge that at that time connected eastern Asia with Alaska's Seward Peninsula, today separated by only 88 km of water.

The migration from Siberia via the Bering Straits took place during the final period of cold that created the last Ice Age. Moisture from the sea, falling as snow, formed the great ice sheet that covered southeastern Alaska and northwestern Canada. The level of the oceans fell several hundred metres, and land bridges emerged.

It is probable that Asian peoples followed migrating herds of animals, such as caribou, giant rodent-like beavers, huge long-horned bison (four times the size of the modern buffalo), and woolly mammoths, back and forth across the two continents. The land bridge was so wide, up to 1600 km in some locations, that to the small bands of Siberian hunters, **Beringia** (the region made up of the former land bridge, the regions west of it in Siberia, and the regions east of it in Alaska and the Yukon) did not seem like a land bridge at all, but a continuation of their

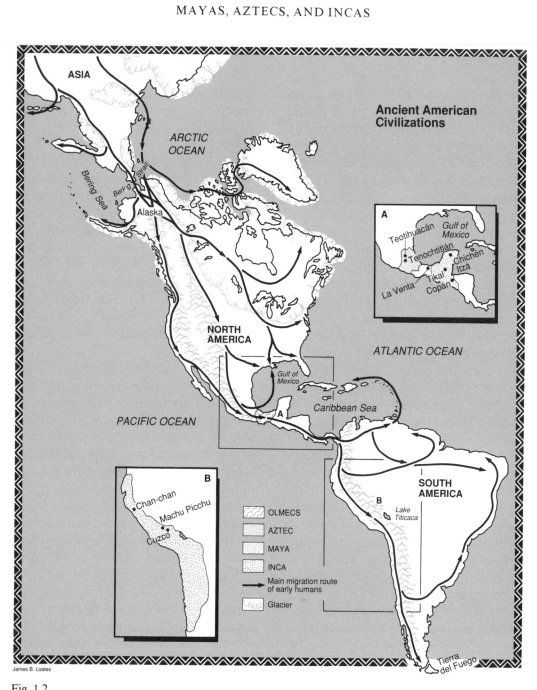

Fig. 1.2
The first inhabitants of the American continent came from Siberia across the Bering Straits.
The map shows the migration routes through North and South America, and the approximate
geographical locations of the major peoples discussed in this book.

hunting grounds. These early migrants had no idea that they were migrating to a separate continent.

Migration was very slow, an entire generation possibly travelling no more than a few kilometres. These migrating bands eventually settled throughout North and Central America. Some even reached the Andes Mountains of South America. Approximately 10 000 years ago, the glaciers began to melt as temperatures warmed. Because of this climatic change, the mammoth, mastodon, giant bison, and other large animals began to disappear, causing the hunting migrations to end. The Bering Land Bridge finally disappeared as the sea level rose again, isolating these first Americans from their ancestral homes.

THE EVIDENCE

Archaeological evidence for the Bering Straits crossing includes findings at a site called Onion Portage, approximately 160 km inland from Alaska's west coast, on the Kobruk River. Fifty different occupation levels, extending over a period of 9000 years, have been discovered at this site. Archaeologists refer to the different levels as **strata**; the lowest levels of occupation are the oldest, the higher levels those more recently occupied.

At the lowest level have been found blades, projectile points, and other chipped tools resembling those found in central Siberia dating from the same time period. These Siberian artifacts belonged to the big-game hunters who roamed Asia between 10 000 and 8000 B.C.E. Many different levels above the lowest recount the history of countless migrations back and forth across

this portage. These migrations occurred in two main waves, one of which included the ancestors of the Amerindians of this hemisphere, and a later one the ancestors of the Inuit. The many differences among Amerindian tribes, with their great variety and contrast in physical features and in culture, are attributed by anthropologists to gradual bodily and cultural adaptations occurring in vastly different environments as these migrants spread out across the Americas.

Other evidence for the central Asian origin of the Amerindian peoples includes the physical resemblance between western hemisphere Amerindians and central Siberians, even to this day, so many hundreds of generations after the migration. As well, Arizona State University archaeologist Cristy Turner has made a study of prehistoric New World human teeth, the most durable of human remains, and has shown them to be like northeast Asian human teeth, and distinguishable from other human teeth anywhere else in the world. Careful scientific and linguistic analyses of folk tales and folk traditions also reveal similarities in culture between the two regions.

FROM HUNTERS TO FARMERS

These early people wandered North and South America for several **millennia** in small bands, hunting and gathering food. Wearing animal skins and using crude stone tools and flint-tipped spears, they hunted and ate meat from animals now extinct in the Americas, such as camels, mastodons, and mammoths. This way of life continued until the end of the last Ice Age some 9000 to 11 000 years ago.

What happened then to trigger the change from hunting and gathering to a **sedentary** way of life leading to the development of agriculture is not well understood, and is the subject of much debate among experts. Some archaeologists suggest the climate change caused large game animals gradually to become extinct. Others think that the change from hunting and gathering to farming came about as a result of "overkill" of the large game animals through the introduction of powerful new stone weapons at about the same time as the melting of the glaciers. Archaeologists call these tools **Clovis stone projectile points**, after the town where they were first discovered, Clovis, New Mexico.

The addition of the Clovis point to the hunting arsenal was the first revolution in technology in the New World. It spread rapidly over the two continents, and enabled hunters to kill great mammoths more efficiently; these huge animals were soon hunted to extinction.

Amerindians then became dependent upon hunting smaller game such as rabbit, bear, deer, smaller bison, and a wide variety of insects and snakes. Wild seeds, nuts, and berries became a more important part of the diet of the people. They ceased being entirely nomadic and began to live in caves and overhanging cliffs, or in simple shelters with animal hide and brush-covered poles.

One of the plants they gathered was a wild grass with a tiny seed pod that had an edible kernel inside. In time, these people somehow learned to make this wild grass produce larger cobs and kernels. This process is known as **domestication**. The domestication of corn is one of the greatest achieve-

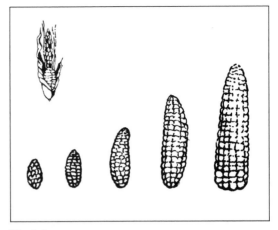

Fig. 1.3
Early forms of corn were much smaller than our corn of today. Wild grasses with large kernels were cross-bred to increase the size of their edible kernels. This process is called hybridization. Cobs as large as our modern corn had been produced by about 1000 B.C.E.

ments of the Americas. Eventually other crops, unknown outside the Americas, such as avocados, beans, chili peppers, squash, tobacco, and tomatoes were also domesticated in different areas. The early Americans had become farmers, living a settled existence. A turning point in pre-Columbian history had been achieved.

AGRICULTURAL SOCIETY

In the western hemisphere the development of agriculture occurred at two separate locations, within a few centuries of each other. The first was in the Andes Mountains located in today's nations of Peru, Ecuador, and Colombia. The second was in the region archaeologists call **Mesoamerica**, the countries today of Guatemala, El Salvador, Belize, the southern part of Mexico, and the northern region of Honduras. Maize, or corn, became the first staple crop, although it may not have been the very first one to be domesticated.

It has been conclusively established that corn was cultivated in the area south of the valley of Mexico by 3500 B.C.E. at the latest, and possibly as early as 5000 B.C.E. The domestication of other crops followed, and by 2000 B.C.E. an agricultural economy had spread throughout Mesoamerica. Corn, beans, and squash eventually formed the basis of the diet in Mesoamerica; many wild edible plants such as chili peppers and pumpkins were also eaten. In the Andean region sweet potatoes and peanuts grew, along with other edible crops. In the end, however, it was corn, easy to grow and hybridize and needing little care, that became the main crop of Mesoamerica and later North America. As a *staple* food it became the equivalent of rice in Asia and wheat in Europe.

A hunting and gathering culture often has an insecure existence, dependent upon skill and luck in foraging for wild plants and hunting its prey. By contrast a farming society has a measure of security, knowing its labour will, in time, produce a dependable food supply. This security and certainty enables the people of a farming society to settle in one place, build permanent homes, and give consideration to other aspects of life besides mere survival. Thus, the cultivation of cereal grain in the Americas became the basis for the beginnings of civilization.

Probably this great change to an agricultural society occurred gradually, as the animals of the hunt disappeared, but it brought about incalculable changes in human lives. Eventually people were able to produce sufficient, even surplus, food without having to spend all their time providing for themselves. They had a new commodity — the precious commodity of time. Time to think about such things as the forces of nature that influenced the fertility of their plants and animals.

The archaeological record shows evidence of the growth of religious practices at this time, practices concerning rituals, gods, and cults paying homage to forces that influence weather. Amerindians began to meditate upon the seasons and to contemplate the gods who provided such bounty, and occasionally, such caprice. They began to build permanent structures, weave cloth, dig for minerals, establish trade, indeed to do all the things required for building a civilization. Other characteristics of more complex societies began to appear in communities as they grew in size. Hereditary rulers and powerful priests, possibly one and the same person, appeared, and temples and palaces were built.

THE FIRST CIVILIZATION OF MESOAMERICA: THE OLMECS

The many groups in Mesoamerica differed in many ways from each other, but they also shared certain aspects of culture not found anywhere else. They all shared a belief in a heaven and an underworld, and worshipped a rain god and a heroic god in human form, known as "Feathered Serpent." Another common feature of these cultures was a hieroglyphic or pictorial form of writing on bark and deerskin paper. To make a book, this bark or paper would be folded like a screen. All groups in the region played a type of sacred ball game on a court, had a fairly complex calendar, practised self-mutilation, and used cacao beans as money. All prepared corn by soaking the cob in lime and water, hand grinding it into dough with a stone, and forming it into a flat cake mixed with red or black kidney beans, called a *tortilla*. It is logical to conclude that the peoples of Mesoamerica shared a common origin now lost, possibly forever. It is also probable that they continued to share ideas over the centuries.

The first known civilization in the region arose in 1200 B.C.E. This was a mysterious people known to history as the Olmecs, a name given to them, long after their disappearance, by other Amerindian people. The name Olmecs means "dwellers from where the rubber grows." It is thought by many scholars that they may have been the civilization from which all subsequent Mesoamerican civilizations received their main ideas. They have been called, by the noted Mesoamerican archaeologist Michael Coe, the "great civilizing force" in Mesoamerica, and the region's first complex society.

Though the Olmecs left behind many artifacts, from massive sculptures to tiny jade pendants, much about these people remains a mystery. They seem to have been dominated by a belief in magic as the cause for the catastrophes in nature that afflict an agricultural people, such as volcanoes, frost, and drought. Those who seemed most able to understand and manipulate the magic exercised control in their society as chieftains. These chieftains, functioning both as kings and priests, were honoured by the Olmec peasantry with gifts, feasts, occasional human sacrifices, and the mobilization of thousands of labourers to build massive sculptures and construct huge pyramids, comparable to those in Egypt. Olmec tributes to their gods and chieftains were the first great artforms of Mesoamerica.

The artifacts that survive from the Olmecs reveal a contradictory view of life and nature. Some of their figurines show grotesque human forms with cleft skulls, pointed heads, or glandular and genital deformities, usually on squat, obese bodies. In contrast other sculptures, like the famous wrestler, portray the beauty of the human form. The Olmecs also left giant stone heads, standing up to three metres high and with a mass of up to twenty tonnes, carved from a rock called basalt. These giant heads had to be moved by the Olmec people over 100 km from their quarries to the sites where they were found. How this was done remains a mystery, as the Olmecs had no animals to act as beasts of burden, and did not use the wheel.

Like the Chinese emperors, the Olmec rulers valued the green stone, jade, above all else. Jade was not found in the Olmec heartland, so the rulers sent traders to distant sites, to the Pacific Ocean, north to Honduras, and into the central valley of Mexico. Through this trade Olmec influence spread throughout Mesoamerica.

Many important cultural legacies from the Olmecs enriched all of the Mesoamerican civilizations that followed. In addition to their art, they seem to have been the first to develop the ability to make rub-

Fig. 1.4
The Olmecs travelled widely in Central America in search of jade. They had a strong impact on the cultures they encountered. They carved colossal stone heads and tiny jade figurines, all showing great artistic ability and sensibility. The Olmecs are now credited with being the founders of civilization in Central America.

ber, to weave cotton into cloth, to make beautiful feather costumes, to master the art of stone-cutting, to build pyramids, and to produce elaborate pottery. They bequeathed a religion, adopted by later civilizations, based upon bloodletting and sacrifice. Burial sites show mutilated skeletons, decapitated skulls, amputated limbs, and murdered children. The calendar, hieroglyphic writing, and the sacred ball game, played with a rubberized ball throughout Mesoamerica, also seem to have originated with the Olmecs.

The Olmec pattern of settlement became the established pattern for the region. The elite class of rulers, nobles, and priests lived in an urban centre. Common people who supplied the labour needed to build the fabulous pyramids, temples, and palaces of the elite lived in the surrounding region. Each centre had a market to distribute agricultural produce and other products. The pattern of settlement remained essentially unchanged until the Spanish conquest in the sixteenth century.

Around 900 B.C.E. the Olmec civilization ended, perhaps because magic and the increasing incidence of violent human sacrifice failed to produce whatever was the desired result. The Olmecs went on an orgy of destruction, smashing monuments, mutilating and burying some of the giant statues face down, and decapitating others. Some experts see this as the result of a peasant revolution, but there is no concrete evidence. The Olmec civilization ultimately disappeared; the people were absorbed into nearby populations.

The true importance of Olmec culture was not realized until the 1920s, when archaeologists began to uncover Olmec artifacts. As the process of discovering Olmec civilization continues, cultural advances that had been previously attributed to later people are credited to these people, whose true name we will likely never learn.

LATER CIVILIZATIONS

In the centuries after the fall of the Olmecs, the population in Mesoamerica continued to grow, and many urban centres sprang up.

One overlooking the Oaxaca Valley in Mexico, **Monte Albán**, the capital of the *Zapotec* civilization, was one of the earliest locations of *glyph* or picture writing carved on stone. This city had a population of 5 000, and controlled most of the heavily populated surrounding villages overlooked by its mountain location. With the use of irrigation and terraced fields, and with the blessings of a well-organized government during a time of peace, the Zapotec population of Monte Albán grew to nearly 20 000 by 200 B.C.E. By 150 B.C.E. the Zapotec centre at Monte Albán had a population that reached 24 000, with large stone buildings, a ball court, and astronomical observatories. This centre remained important until around 700 C.E. when, like other centres in Mesoamerica before and after, it mysteriously collapsed.

During the first centuries C.E., three advanced civilizations developed in three distinct regions of the western hemisphere. In the central valley of Mexico a great urban centre was constructed at **Teotihuacán**. Teotihuacán was the sixth largest urban area in the world at that time, and the only city in the western hemisphere comparable to European and Asian cities. Some have compared the city with Imperial Rome as a political, economic, religious, and cultural centre. Not only was it the first real city in North America, but no pre-Columbian city compared with it in size or influence, even those built by the great city-building civilization of the Maya.

Teotihuacán was North America's first planned city, covering some twenty square kilometres. Estimates of the city's population at the peak of its influence during the sixth century range from 125 000 to 200 000. It was dominated by two magnificent pyramids, the Pyramid of the Moon and the Pyramid of the Sun, connected by a large concourse called the Avenue of the Dead. The Pyramid of the Sun was almost as large as the greatest pyramid of Egypt, the Pyramid of Kufu, and until the twentieth century, even as a ruin it was one of the largest buildings in all North America.

Teotihuacán seems to have been the cultural and religious centre of the Mesoamerican region for 700 years. After 700 C.E. it faded in importance, leaving little cultural trace, for reasons still disputed. Experts speculate about the possibility of natural disaster or crop failure; skeletal remains from the time of collapse show much disease. Given the immensity of the labour put into pyramid building, there may have been a violent political revolution; there is evidence of a great fire in the city centre around 700 C.E., possibly caused by rebellion or invasion. Murals on palace walls begin to show military themes for the first time around 600 C.E., lending credence to this theory. The collapse of Teotihuacán opened Mexico to less civilized tribes from the north, one of whom was the Mexica, better known to history as the Aztecs, and the subject of Chapter 3.

At the same time as Teotihuacán dominated Mexico's central valley, the early **Maya** were beginning to construct many urban centres, stretching from southern Mexico to the highlands of Guatemala. Near today's Guatemala City the large urban centre of **Kaminaljuyú** reached its peak around 500 B.C.E. In the same region **Tikal, El Mirador**, and **Izapa** also became impor-

Fig. 1.5
The Pyramid of the Sun at Teotihuacán, with terraced slopes, rises more than sixty metres high. The platforms in the foreground were probably temples which led up to the Pyramid of the Sun.

tant urban centres. Further south, in the Andes Mountains near Lake Titicaca, the **Tiahuanaco** civilization built an urban centre of colossal stone architecture and huge statues. This site was a centre of civilization for over 1400 years; and yet the people and cultures that inhabited it at different times remain for the most part an enigma. The story of the Mayan civilization will be described in Chapter 2 and that of Tiahuanaco in Chapter 4.

Until recently we knew little about the circumstances of the rise of these civiliza-tions or the purposes of their urban centres. As well, the reasons for their decline and fall were not well understood. They seemed to have arisen mysteriously, with no obvious connecting link between their sophisticated urban inhabitants and the prehistoric people who preceded them. Modern archaeology, through such methods as the translation of previously undecipherable glyphs and the discovery of more artifacts, is slowly adding new pieces towards the solution of the puzzle.

By the time of the Spanish arrival, all

these civilizations were dead, their urban centres long deserted and overgrown, and their sites a mystery even to the Amerindians encountered by the Spaniards. In approaching a study of these fascinating peoples we must realize that there are virtually no written records to help the student of pre-Columbian history, as no inhabitant of pre-Columbian North or South America ever wrote a paragraph or a sentence as we would conceive of it. In addition, there are almost no records of any single individual from these early civilizations. Therefore, in studying the subjects of the next three chapters of this book, it must be realized that the archaeologist and historian are at a disadvantage when compared with those who study, for example, the roots of European cultures, where such records, if not plentiful, at least exist. Nevertheless the road ahead is exciting, as there is much that has been discovered in recent years about these fascinating peoples and their intriguing civilizations, and more new information is being uncovered every year.

HIGHLIGHTS

1. Nomadic hunters crossed to the Americas, by way of a Bering Straits land bridge, anywhere from 12 000 to 40 000 years ago.
2. These early hunters wandered for thousands of years before they reached Mexico and farther south, some even crossing into South America and settling in the Andean Highlands.
3. At some point these Amerindians began to change from hunters and gatherers to simple farmers. This may have occurred about 9 000 years ago, after large game animals became extinct because of climatic change and the introduction of new and more efficient weapons.
4. This change was gradual, the chief food changing from small animals and birds to domesticated plants such as corn, avocados, squash, beans, and chili peppers.
5. The domestication of plants enabled societies to devote more of their time to constructing permanent settlements and to developing religions.
6. One important early group was the Olmecs, who developed much of what was later used by other civilizations, including hieroglyphics, the calendar, and the ability to make rubber and to weave cloth.
7. In the first few centuries C.E. urban centres began to appear in three locations: at Teotihuacán in central Mexico, at several Mayan sites in Mesoamerica, and in the central Andean mountain region.

TERMS TO UNDERSTAND

Write a one-sentence explanation of each of the following terms. Write a sentence using each word.

domestication
ethnocentrism
indigenous
Mesoamerica
millennia
pre-Columbian
precursor
sedentary
strata

RELATED TOPICS FOR RESEARCH AND PRESENTATION

Pyramids of the Americas

The legend of Atlantis

The legend of the sixth century transatlantic voyage of the Irish monk St. Brendan

The Kon-Tiki Expedition

The giant stones of Easter Island

The origin of agriculture

The mound building Indians of Poverty Point, Mississippi

The mound building Indians of Ohio

The Pueblo building Anasazi of New Mexico's Chaco Canyon

Shamanism and religion in Latin America today

The civilization of the Olmecs

Monte Albán and the Zapotecs

Teotihuacán and the Pyramids of the Sun and the Moon

The five cities that rose and were abandoned at Tiahuanaco

FOR ADDITIONAL READING AND RESEARCH

Adams, Richard E. W., *Prehistoric Mesoamerica*. Little, Brown, Toronto, 1977.

del Castillo, Bernal Diaz, *The Discovery and Conquest of Mexico, 1517- 1521*. Octagon Books, New York, 1970.

Ceram, C. W., ed., *The First American: A Story of North American Archeology*. Harcourt Brace Jovanovich, New York, 1971.

Claiborne, Robert, and the Editors of Time-Life Books, *The Emergence of Man: The First Americans*. Time-Life Books, New York, 1973.

Coe, Michael D., *America's First Civilization, Discovering the Olmecs*. American Heritage Publishing, New York, 1968.

Coe, Michael, Dean Snow and Elizabeth Benson, *Atlas of Ancient America*. Facts On File Publications, New York, 1986.

Dickey, Thomas, Vance Muse, and Henry Wiencek, *The God-Kings of Mexico*. Stonehenge Press, Chicago, 1982.

Fagan, Brian M., *The Great Journey, The Peopling of Ancient America*. Thames and Hudson, New York, 1987.

Fiedel, Stuart J., *Prehistory of the Americas*. Cambridge University Press, Cambridge, 1987.

Fisher, Leonard Everett, *Pyramid of the Sun, Pyramid of the Moon*. Macmillan, 1988.

Heiser, Charles B., Jr., *Seed to Civilization: The Story of Man's Food*. W. H. Freeman, San Francisco, 1973.

Highwater, Jamake, *Native Land-Sagas of the Indian Americas*. Little, Brown, Toronto, 1986.

Heyerdahl, Thor, *Kon-Tiki*. Rand McNally, Skokie, Illinois, 1950.

Heyerdahl, Thor, *Early man and the Oceans*. Random House of Canada, 1978.

Hopkins, D. M., *The Bering Land Bridge*. Stanford University Press, Palo Alto, 1987.

Katz, Friedrich, *The Ancient American Civilizations*. Weidenfeld and Nicolson, London, 1969.

Leonard, Jonathon N., *Ancient America*. Time-Life Books, New York, 1967.

Littmann, Mark, *Skywatchers of Ancient Mexico*. Hansen Planetarium, Salt Lake City, Utah, 1982.

McIntosh, Jane, *The Practical Archaeologist, How we know what we know about the past*. Facts on File Publications, New York, 1986.

Meyer, Karl E., *Teotihuacán*. Newsweek. New York, 1973.

Miller, Mary Ellen, *The Art of Mesoamerica, From Olmec to Aztec*. Thames and Hudson, London, 1986.

Mysteries of the Ancient Americas, The New World Before Columbus. Reader's Digest, Pleasantville, New York, 1986.

Pike, Donald G., *Anasazi: Ancient People of the Rock.* Crown Publishers, 1974.

Severin, Tim, *The Brendan Voyage.* McGraw-Hill, New York, 1978.

Silverberg, Robert, *Mound Builders of Ancient America: The Archaeology of a Myth.* Graphic Society, Greenwich, Conn., 1968.

Soustelle, Jacques, *The Olmecs, The Oldest Civilization in Mexico.* Doubleday, Garden City, New York, 1984.

Stuart, Gene S., *America's Ancient Cities.* National Geographic Society, Washington D. C., 1988.

Tompkins, Peter, *Mysteries of the Mexican Pyramids.* Harper and Row, New York, 1976.

Weaver, Muriel Porter, *The Aztecs, Maya, and their Predecessors.* Harcourt Brace Jovanovich, New York, 1972.

West, Frederick Hadleigh, *The Archaeology of Beringia.* Columbia University Press, New York, 1981.

The World's Last Mysteries. Reader's Digest, Pleasantville, New York, 1978.

CHAPTER TWO

THE MAYA

The Maya created an advanced civilization in the tropical rainforests and highlands of Mesoamerica between the third and tenth centuries of the Common Era. They built a network of populous cities with beautiful pyramid-topped temples and palaces, accomplishing this without the benefit of metal, the wheel, or beasts of burden. They developed advanced systems of mathematics and astronomy, and a beautiful art of great sophistication. Yet they also practised human sacrifice and self-torture, and they fought continuously amongst themselves. Suddenly and mysteriously, at the height of its greatness, this civilization collapsed. City after city was abandoned, and the people were reduced to a simpler way of life.

INTRODUCTION

When the Spanish **conquistadores** arrived in the New World at the end of the fifteenth century, hidden deep within the forests were abandoned cities built of stone, with giant pyramids and great palaces, all grown over with trees and brush. The **Maya** who built these cities had disappeared long before the arrival of the Spanish, the people having mysteriously abandoned their urban centres between approximately the ninth and tenth century C.E. In many cases buildings had been abandoned in mid-construction, leaving huge and fabulous murals half finished. The rea-

son for this abandonment of the Mayan centres of civilization remains puzzling and is the subject of much debate.

The Maya during the **Classic Period** of their history had the most advanced and the only completely literate civilization on the American continent. In fact their achievements were equalled by very few peoples at any time before our own period. The roots of Mayan culture probably extended as far back as the fifth millennium B.C.E., but the "Classic Period" of its greatness lasted approximately between 300 and 900 C.E. The Maya produced great astronomers, scientists, and mathematicians during this time, which was the period of Europe's "Dark Ages." As well, the Maya produced great

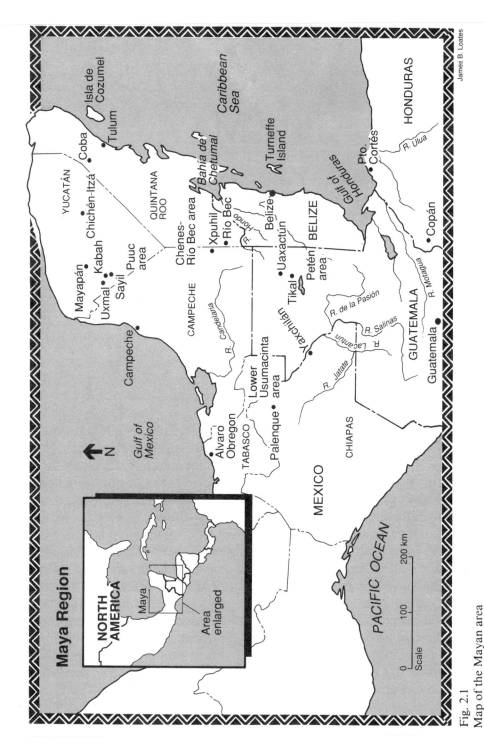

James B. Loates

Fig. 2.1
Map of the Mayan area

artists, architects, and builders. Mayan roads have been favourably compared to Roman roads, and the Mayan calendar and counting systems were the best in the world, unequalled anywhere for many centuries. In addition, the Maya developed a system of writing, based on idea-pictures called **glyphs**, that was far superior to all other pre-Columbian writing systems, either before or after the Mayan period of history.

The Maya Classic Period was centred in southern Mayan cities such as Copan, Tikal, and Palenque. After the mysterious collapse of these and other southern cities at the end of the Classic Period, the centre of Mayan civilization moved northwards into the Yucatán peninsula and regions nearby. Here a second flowering of culture occurred at such sites as Chichén-Itzá and Mani. During this later period Mayan culture appears to have been heavily influenced by the more warlike Toltec people of Mexico. These northern sites too, mysteriously declined in the thirteenth century, Chichén-Itzá being abandoned about 1224 C.E.

The remnants of Mayan civilization were not understood or appreciated by the Spanish invaders and conquerors of the sixteenth century. No doubt we would know much more of this civilization's greatness had not overzealous Spanish priests burned virtually all of the Mayan books, books they saw as dangerously filled with pagan ideas. Only three books seem to have survived this grievous annihilation of learning and ideas. The reckless destruction of centuries of Mayan learning is one of the great tragedies in history.

The wholesale burning of Mayan books, called **codices**, destroyed forever the possibility of making a complete study of these marvellous people. The study of the Maya now has to be based on archaeological studies, the three remaining books, dealing mainly with astronomy and religion, and a few accounts left by the Spanish churchmen of the sixteenth century, men who little understood the grandeur of the Mayan civilization. Except for these churchmen, the Classic Period Maya were a people and a civilization virtually forgotten by the entire world for a thousand years.

THE REDISCOVERY OF THE MAYA

In 1839 President Martin Van Buren of the United States sent a young diplomat named John Lloyd Stephens to the Yucatán and Central America. His mission was to establish contact between the government of the United States and the newly independent and strife-torn governments of Central America. But Stephens' first love was archaeology, and the real purpose of his mission was to explore the reports of ruins of ancient cities in Central and South America.

Accompanying Stephens was a British artist and architect named Frederick Catherwood. An older man than Stephens, Catherwood had explored the ancient cities of Egypt and the Near East, and had made meticulous drawings of ancient Egyptian, Greek, and Roman art and architecture. Stephens, aware that he would need proof of any findings, had asked Catherwood if he would go with him to the jungle.

Stephens had earlier come upon a book about "lost" Mayan cities of the Yucatán

Fig. 2.2
John Lloyd Stephens

peninsula and had become fascinated by this forgotten civilization. He searched out everything he could find on the subject in New York City, which amounted to very little in the 1830s, only a few books and articles. These described many ruined cities and the rumours of many more, covered by forbidding jungle growth. At the time most people believed these ruins were of little importance; they thought that the Amerindian had never risen above a state of semi-savagery, and had been unable at any time in the past to construct anything remotely resembling a civilization. There had been few archaeological excavations on any Amerindian site, and little had been revealed of the earlier achievements of Amerindian civilizations.

With local guides and pack mules, Stephens and Catherwood set out in 1839 on an arduous journey across Mico Mountain in the war-torn country of Honduras. Both the physical hardships of the climb up the steep, muddy slope, and the political danger from opposing factions in the Honduran civil war threatened the success of their journey. After escaping danger narrowly on more than one occasion, the two men finally hacked their way through the jungle and into the previously unknown city of **Copán**. What they found was beyond their wildest expectations.

Before them lay the ruins of a huge pyramid. The ground around it was strewn with broken stone images of serpents, jaguars, unknown animals, and human figures, all partially or completely buried by earth and growing plants. The pyramid was capped by a row of death's heads, and in front of it stood gigantic stone jaguars. At the very top of the pyramid the huge head of a god looked out over the remains. This desolate and deserted ruin had been covered by jungle for a millennium. Only spider monkeys inhabited the place. The lost world of the Classic Period Maya, after a thousand years of neglect, had finally been rediscovered.

Catherwood immediately sketched what they had found. The artist, often in conditions of heavy rain, in poor light, standing in deep mud while fighting off mosquitoes, carefully drew the rest of their discoveries as Stephens and Amerindian workmen measured, surveyed, and mapped the site. After working under these conditions for two weeks, the rough outline of ancient Copán began to emerge. In the centre of a large plaza, surrounded by five other plazas and other outlying districts, was a huge pyramid with a flat summit, surrounded by smaller pyramids and temples. At one corner of the complex stood the Hieroglyphic Stairway, which climbed up an enormous pyramid; each of its 63 steps was carved with undecipherable Mayan writing, called hieroglyphs. In the words of Stephens:

"savages never reared these structures, savages never carved these stones . . . orators, warriors, and statesmen, beauty, ambition, and glory had lived and passed away . . . here."

Together Stephens and Catherwood explored some 44 Mayan ruins in journeys to the jungle interior between 1839 and 1842. Often they travelled on muleback, usually during the difficult rainy season, through dense jungle footpaths. The two explorers had to dismount in many treacherous locations to be carried by their fearful Amerindian guides. At the time of their discovery of the fabulous city of **Palenque**, sometimes considered the most beautiful Mayan city of all, they were plagued by ten days of continuous, heavy rain that rusted their equipment and ruined their clothing, food, and artists' supplies. Here Stephens wrote:

"In the romance of the world's history, nothing ever impressed me more forcibly than the spectacle of this once great and lovely city, overturned, desolate, and lost; discovered by accident, overgrown with trees, it did not even have a name to distinguish it."

They had a little easier time at **Chichén-Itzá**, a Mayan ruin near the sea and accessible by a good road. In this marvellous ruin they found the Temple of the Warriors, guarded by the mysterious figure of the grimacing *Chacmool*. Here they also found a

"sacred ball court," a circular astronomical observatory, and many other beautiful buildings. They also found fabulous sculptures of serpent heads and high, stepped pyramids capped by temples, such as the one pictured.

"At four o'clock we left Piste, and very soon we saw rising high above the plain the Castillo of Chichén. In half an hour we were among the ruins of the ancient city, with all the great buildings in full view, casting prodigious shadows over the plain, and presenting a spectacle which, even after all that we had seen, once more excited in us emotions of wonder . . . I know that it is impossible by any narrative to convey to the reader a true idea of the powerful and exciting interest of wandering (among ancient lost cities) . . . They give an entirely new aspect to the great continent on which we live, and bring up with more force than ever the great question . . . : Who were the builders of these American cities?"

Later the travellers published two lavishly illustrated books of their visits to these 44 Mayan cities. These books caused scholars and historians to reassess these sites and the level of pre-Columbian Amerindian civilizations. The books also were popular reading among the general public of the time, and Stephens became the "father of Mayan archaeology" for his contributions to the reawakening of interest in Mayan civilization. His books have become classics, and are still often read and reread even today by people interested in history and adventure.

Fig. 2.3
Catherwood's illustration of Chichén-Itzá, as it looked when he first saw it in 1841, overgrown with jungle.

MAYA ORIGINS

Much has been learned about the Maya since the time of Stephens and Catherwood. Archaeologists have systematically excavated numerous Mayan cities, and the history and culture of these fascinating people has begun to take shape. Archaeologists have been helped to understand the Mayan world by the work of linguists, geologists, naturalists, and experts from other related fields.

Many experts now believe the first Maya were a small group of people who migrated from the Pacific Coast of what is now the United States sometime around the third millennium B.C.E. Their first identifiable location was on the highly fertile Gulf coastal plain of Mexico and northern Belize. Here they established Stone Age villages, lived in simple thatch huts, and used spears, scrapers, drills, needles made from bone and antler, and millstones for grinding

food. This fertile land was planted with corn and produced great surpluses probably unmatched anywhere in the New World to that time. The people were therefore able to turn to cultural pursuits. Many features of this culture seem to have evolved from the earlier Olmec culture. All this occurred sometime during the first centuries of the Common Era, and is known as the Mayan **Pre-Classic Period** of history.

As the Mayan population grew, different social classes developed, including hereditary rulers and a powerful and influential priestly class, both dominating the masses of illiterate peasants. Villages developed from small farming settlements into important religious and economic centres. Stone temples and palaces were constructed, hieroglyph writing began , a calendar was developed by a process called *calendrics*, and advanced and sophisticated art forms evolved. Exactly when and how all these changes took place remains unclear. Not long after this initial prosperity, the Maya expanded inland to the northern areas of Central America. It was here that the first "great" civilization of the New World began in the early years of the fourth century C.E.

THE CLASSIC PERIOD

The centuries between approximately 325 C.E. and 925 C.E. are referred to by historians as the **Classic Period** of the Maya; this period was the culmination of several centuries of extraordinary progress. More than one writer on this subject has compared the Maya to the ancient Greeks, and concluded that because of their great accomplishments, unrivalled in many fields of culture, the Maya could be called the "Greeks of the New World." Older histories of the Maya also thought that Mayan society was a peaceable one like the Greek, but this view has been substantially revised. Recent discoveries and newly deciphered glyphs clearly show the Mayan city-states were frequently involved in conflict and conquest,

and were anything but peaceable.

Compared with all other pre-Columbian civilizations, the Maya of the Classic Period made great advances in painting, architecture, sculpture, mathematics, glyph writing, history, and astronomy. Their architecture was magnificent in scale, with beautiful stonework and sculpture. They had outstanding jadework, featherwork, and woodwork. They made pottery comparable in its beauty to any ever produced, and they made it without the basic potter's tool — the potter's wheel. At the very end of the Classic Period metals began to play an important role in Mayan life. Excavations have revealed many copper objects from about 900 C.E., including axes, tweezers, and bells. Gold ornaments such as rings and cups have also been found. Overall the Mayan accomplishments during the Classic Period were unequalled before or after in the pre-Columbian world. The later civilizations of the Incas and Aztecs surpassed them only in political and military development and in the extent of their empires.

CHRONOLOGY OF MAYAN HISTORY

600 B.C.E. TO 300 C.E.	FORMATIVE OR PRE-CLASSIC PERIOD first Maya centres appear in Tikal, Copán, other sites
300 C.E. TO 900 C.E.	CLASSIC PERIOD great flowering of Mayan civilizations; peak reached in Late Classic at Copán, Tikal, and Palenque
900 C.E. TO 1300 C.E.	POST-CLASSIC PERIOD rapid decline and abandonment of Mayan city-states; later Mayan/Toltec Chichén-Itzá revival of culture

PHYSICAL APPEARANCE AND CLOTHING

Artifacts that survive from the ancient Mayas picture the people as short and stocky in build, with broad, sloping foreheads, full lips with the lower lip turned down, medium brown to copper-coloured skin, dark, almond-shaped eyes, high cheekbones, and high-bridged, prominent noses. The Maya of the Yucatán region today are similar in physical appearance, and are likely descendants of these ancient people. It should be noted that the Mayas thought that a forehead that sloped back abruptly from the top of the eyebrows was far more attractive than a straight one, and so would place the soft skull of a newborn baby between two flat boards until it hardened into a flat, sloping forehead in front and a flat, straight head at the back. It should also be noted that a crosseyed squint was considered beautiful, and so mothers would tie small beads or balls in front of a child. The child would watch the dangling objects and eventually become crosseyed.

Because of the year-round high humidity in Mesoamerica, the Maya dressed for adornment, not for warmth. Cotton, one of the few crops in common in both the New and the Old World, was grown, spun into thread, and dyed with bright colours extracted from berries and insects. The Maya also decorated themselves with jade beads, multicoloured sea shells, and feathers.

There was a notable difference between the clothing of the Mayan nobility and of the common people. The nobility dressed ornately, especially during religious cere-monies. They wore sandals made of deer hide or jaguar skin tied with vegetable fibre, and long capes made from jaguar skins. They were fond of trimming capes and head-dresses with the feathers of the sacred quetzal bird, which are a beautiful shade of turquoise. Other head-dresses were made from animal or snake heads. A male noble would wear a belt with a variety of animal skulls dangling from it.

The Mayan nobility also wore a great deal of jewelry, made usually from jade, the green colour of which represented life, and was associated with the lush and fertile tropical forests surrounding them. They also made jewelry from bone, stones, and wood, occasionally from feathers, and later in their history they began to use gold, copper, and silver in jewelry making. The final destination of most of this jewelry was the grave, as the jewelry accompanied its dead owner to the next world.

Women had jewelry dangling in their pierced ears and noses; men would remove the hair from the front of their heads by singeing it off. (There is no evidence that the Maya had any type of scissors, so that burning off the hair was the most effective way of removing it.) The men would then grow their hair from the middle of their heads down their backs, braid it, roll it up in a colourful cotton band, and tie it on the top of their head with a strip of fabric.

The Mayan lower classes wore a simple cotton loincloth and a sleeveless jacket made from cotton. They also wore a thin cape tied in a knot at the left shoulder. The women wore a shapeless cotton skirt and were covered by a shawl. Women wore braided hair decorated with jade or shells.

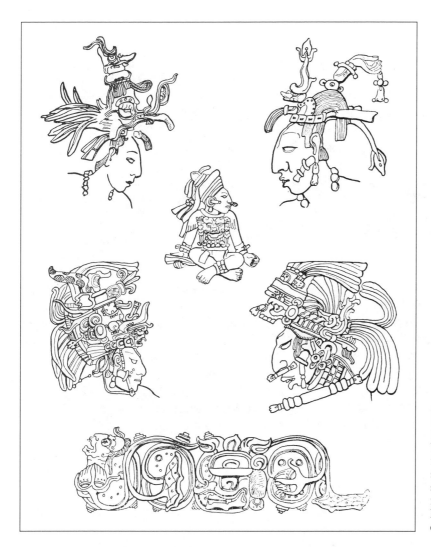

Fig. 2.4
Mayan conceptions of beauty included the features shown here: the sloped forehead, almond-shaped eyes, prominent nose, slightly pouting lower lip, and receding chin.

Men and women occasionally wore sandals made from deerskin or fibre, but more often went barefoot. Both sexes filed their teeth to points and studded them with jade pieces. Both used perfumes, tattoos, and body paint; they sometimes carved scars into their skin for decoration.

THE MAYAN CALENDAR

It is not unusual for a civilization dominated by farming and a by a religion that celebrated agricultural festivals to want an exact knowledge of the seasons. Once the Maya had become a settled agricultural people with a need to know when to seed, when to cultivate, when to harvest, and when to store crops, some sort of accurate measurement of time was necessary. But to the Maya, time was not merely a way of ordering events but a religious force involving powerful gods who had the ability to create and destroy. The Maya believed that if they could predict which of these gods were dominant at a particular time, they could better control their destiny. The Maya became obssesed with time, and this obsession led to one of the greatest accomplishments of all ancient civilizations, their exceptionally precise calendar.

Subdivisions of the Mayan calendar such as days, months, and years, were seen as "burdens" to be carried on the backs of the gods. At the end of an allotted subdivision of time, one god gave up its burden to another god, and Mayan actions would be influenced by whether the god receiving the burden would bring a lucky or unlucky period. Since an ability to understand and predict the nature of time was the key to people's fortunes, those with this special knowledge had access to essential information. Therefore, the Mayan conception of time gave great power to the guardians of time — the rulers and priests — over the masses who did not have such knowledge.

Mayan astronomers and mathematicians studied the sun, the moon, and the stars for dozens of generations, and made detailed observations of their movements in the sky. In addition, they had very carefully studied the eclipses of the sun and the moon, and could predict these as well. One of the three Mayan books that survived the Spanish conquest is called the *Dresden Codex*, and when it was deciphered it showed that the

Mayan calculation of the lunar month was amazingly accurate. Such a calculation had to be based on long periods of observing the sun, moon, and stars. The Maya said that 405 full moons would occur over a time period of 11 960 days, and astronomers know today that 405 full moons take place over 11 958.888 days. The Maya were off only 5 minutes a year in their calendar! What makes this even more amazing is that the Maya did all this calculating without any sighting instrument, such as a telescope.

As with our calendar, each Maya year had 365 days, but the year was divided into 18 months or **uinals** of 20 days (**kins**) each, plus one five-day month. These five days were considered very unlucky days, and Mayans stayed in their homes during this time. An extra day was added every four years, just as in our leap year. Individual days do not seem to have had names. There are no findings of subdivisions of the day such as our hours, minutes, or seconds; the kin is the smallest known Mayan time segment. The Maya did not believe that time was **linear**, but **cyclical**, that is, a person could come back to the same time by completing a cycle, so that history repeated itself.

Every 20 years marked a **katun**, or cycle of years, and the five-day month at the end of the katun was the most feared time of all. In an attempt to forestall the end of the world, priests in rain-god costumes climbed to the top of a pyramid, where human sacrifices took place. The victims had their hearts cut out; the hearts were carried in a bowl to a sacred stela and then buried in an adjacent pit. Maya watching the ceremony

Fig. 2.5
The Observatory at Chichén-Itzá, also known as El Carocol. It is generally believed that Mayan astronomers made astronomical sightings from fixed observation points in this tower.

jabbed themselves with sharp sticks and threw them into the same pit.

The Mayan calendar was more accurate than any calendar established by the great civilizations of Greece or Rome, and remained the most accurate in the world until the calendar developed by Pope Gregory a little over 400 years ago, in 1582.

STELAE

The Maya left behind large carvings called **stelae**. These were vertical slabs of stone erected every five, ten, or twenty years in order to record positions of the heavenly bodies and to register eclipses. They were also used to register the names and years of Mayan ruling dynasties. These stelae were usually beautifully decorated with elaborate carvings, and so they serve as a valuable record of Mayan art and history. As we have seen, the Maya believed history repeated itself, and so recording history was extremely important in predicting the future. Many of the surviving stelae are broken, and the surface carvings have been eroded by rains and dense vegetation; but some have been preserved nearly intact.

Fig. 2.6
This stele erected 766 C.E. shows the intricacy and detail of Mayan stone carving.

One of the problems archaeologists face is how to correlate the stelae dates of Mayan years with those of our calendar. The Mayan year was used in a system called the **Long Count**. This system recorded dates from what the Maya believed was the beginning of the most recent cycle, the date of zero, just as the Gregorian calendar that we use records time from the birth of Christ. The Mayan beginning of time is believed by many archaeologists to correspond to our date of 3114 B.C.E. However, not all archaeologists are in agreement on this year, as the translation of Mayan dates is not complete. Still, because the Maya were so precise in recording their history on the stelae, we can understand the sequence of their history even if we cannot be certain of correlating it with other histories in Europe, Asia, and Africa.

THE MAYAN NUMBER SYSTEM

The Mayan fascination with dates and with time led them to develop a number system more advanced than that of either ancient Greece or Rome. Most Mayan numbers that have been found are in the form of dates such as the beginning of their calendar, which, as we have seen, experts believe may correspond to August 11, 3114 B.C.E. Their number system was based on the unit of 20 (**vigesimal**) rather than on our unit of ten (decimal). Possibly the vigesimal system developed from counting fingers and toes, rather than just fingers.

It is very easy to read and use Mayan numbers because the Mayan vigesimal system of numbers worked just as well as our own system. Only three symbols were needed, and unlike the clumsy Roman numeral system or other less advanced numerical systems, there was no need for many repetitions of the same symbol. For example, the number 388 would be written as CCCLXXXVIII in Roman numerals. Mayan numbers are represented by dots and bars. In addition, there is a shell-like symbol representing zero.

The development of the number zero was an important advance in Mesoamerican mathematics. The principle of zero is critical in all but the simplest of calculations. The Arabs were the first people in the Old

As in our number system, the position of each figure is vital: Mayan numbers are not read left to right, horizontally, as our numbers are, but are read from bottom to top, or vertically. For example, to write the number six, the Maya used a dot above the bar • , and the number ten was represented by two bars: ▬▬ .

Some examples of Mayan numbers follow:

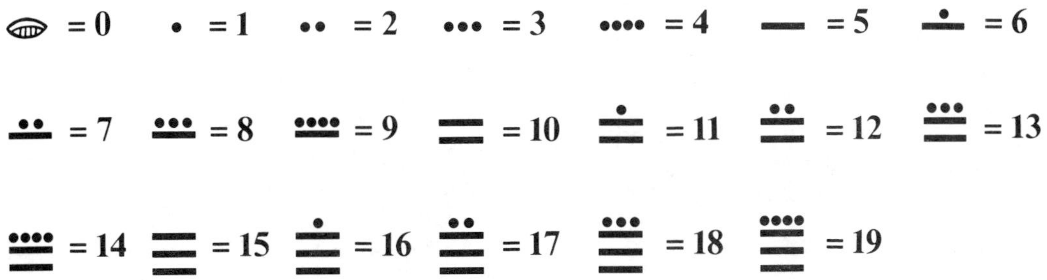

◉ = 0   • = 1   •• = 2   ••• = 3   •••• = 4   ▬ = 5   ▬•▬ = 6

▬••▬ = 7   ▬•••▬ = 8   ▬••••▬ = 9   ▬▬ = 10   ▬•▬ = 11   ▬••▬ = 12   ▬•••▬ = 13

▬••••▬ = 14   ▬▬▬ = 15   ▬•▬ = 16   ▬••▬ = 17   ▬•••▬ = 18   ▬••••▬ = 19

In the decimal system we move one column to the left when the number 10 is reached; in the vigesimal system of the Maya we move one column up (vertically) when we reach 20:

• / ◉ = 20   •• / • = 21   • / •• = 22   • / ••• = 23   • / •••• = 24   ▬ / • = 25

In our number system we would move another column to the left when we reach 100 (or 10×10); the Maya moved up one more column when they reached 400 (20×20) some examples follow:

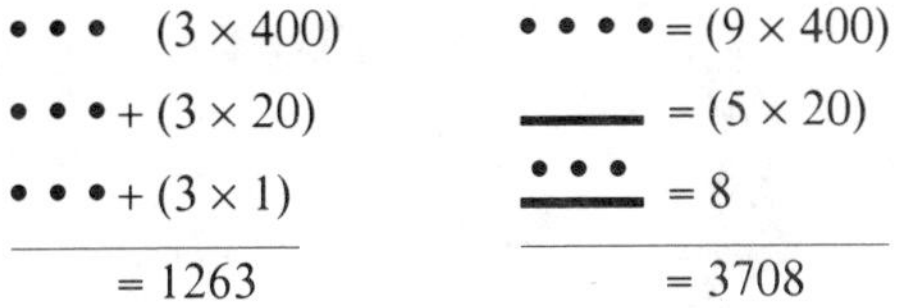

$$\begin{array}{ll} \bullet\bullet\bullet\ (3 \times 400) & \bullet\bullet\bullet\bullet = (9 \times 400) \\ \bullet\bullet\bullet + (3 \times 20) & \text{▬} = (5 \times 20) \\ \bullet\bullet\bullet + (3 \times 1) & \text{▬•••▬} = 8 \\ \hline = 1263 & = 3708 \end{array}$$

As the Maya reached the number 8000 they moved up another rung ($20 \times 20 \times 20$)

See if you can write the following Mayan numbers.

30   67   500   921   1234   8340

Can you read the following Maya numbers:

(a)  [Maya number figure]

(b) 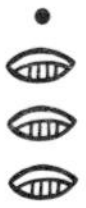 [Maya number figure]

(c) 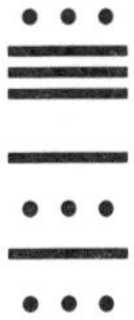 [Maya number figure]

Answers:

(a) 8000
    (2×400)
    (4×20)
    8
    ———
    = 888

(b) 8000

(c) (18×8000)
    (5×400)
    (8×20)
    3
    ———
    = 146 163

Fig. 2.7

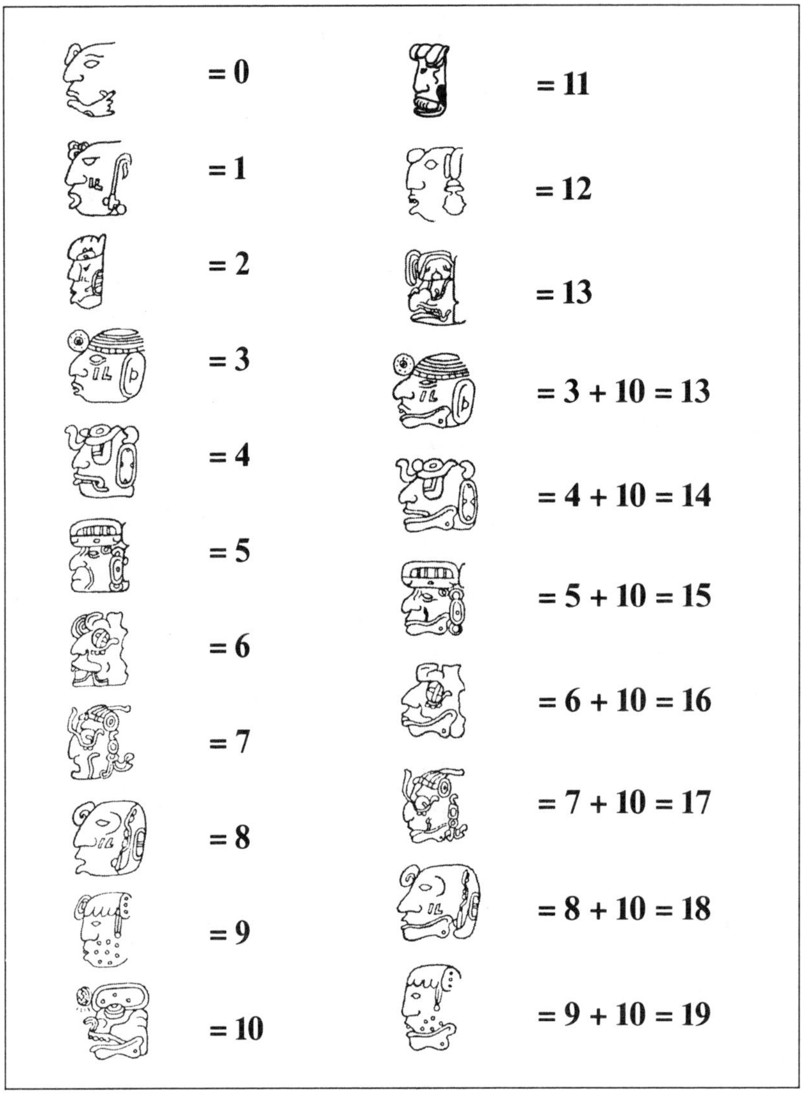

= 0		= 11	
= 1		= 12	
= 2		= 13	
= 3		= 3 + 10 = 13	
= 4		= 4 + 10 = 14	
= 5		= 5 + 10 = 15	
= 6		= 6 + 10 = 16	
= 7		= 7 + 10 = 17	
= 8		= 8 + 10 = 18	
= 9		= 9 + 10 = 19	
= 10			

Fig. 2.8

World to use this concept, and Europeans copied it from them about 1000 years ago, at a time when the ancient people of Meso-america had already been using zero for centuries.

The Maya had a second kind of number system; numbers in this system were represented by highly stylized pictures of the heads of gods or deities. Gods of the sun, rain, death, and others represented the numbers zero to thirteen. After thirteen, the heads were combined together.

WRITING

The Maya did not have a written alphabet. They used a system of picture writing known as *hieroglyphic* writing, which they carved onto walls, columns, stairways, and ornaments. The Maya used about 800 different picture symbols, or glyphs. Mayan writing is unique and cannot be compared to other forms of writing developed elsewhere. Deciphering the meanings of the glyphs has been painfully slow as a result. While progress is being made, many of these symbols remain a mystery. The specialists who work on these glyphs have translated symbols for the days, months, numbers, compass directions, colours, ruling dynasties and gods, but because so much remains to be translated, scholars are only able to understand the main words. Many details, nuances, and subtleties remain undecipherable, not least because the Maya wrote with such decoration that it is often impossible to tell what is a glyph and what is an ornament. Mayan writers seemed not to like any blank spaces and filled them up with decorative art. As a result of the difficulty in deciphering Mayan writing, there is little doubt that much that has been written about the Maya to date will need correcting when more glyphs are understood. Some Mayanists, experts in Mayan studies, optimistically believe that all Mayan glyphs may be understood by the end of this century.

Recently translated glyphs show that the Maya engaged in more violence and human sacrifice than had been earlier believed. They indicate that Maya cities were in a constant state of warfare with each other, the primary goal being to take captives, not to gain territory. The Maya preferred to capture members of the nobility, who were often sacrificed after a long period of torture and mutilation. Glyphs translated from stelae show bloody human sacrifices of captured victims, killed to satisfy gods that needed the victims' blood for nourishment. These captives were sacrificed by priests who decapitated them or sliced their chests open with obsidian blades and tore out their still-beating hearts. Other glyphs show blood dripping from members of the ruling family, who pulled thorny ropes through holes they had cut in their own tongues! Whether this was done as a form of sacrifice or was performed as penitence is unknown.

In 1988 a West German archaeologist named Wolfgang Gockel, working at the Mayan ruin of Palenque, claimed to have deciphered the Mayan glyph system. He has said that Mayan pictures of men, animals, birds, and abstract patterns represent descriptions of struggles for power within Mayan society. These struggles took place at court, in war, and during natural disasters. The findings also paint a picture of a highly complex and structured society. Most of the glyphs, according to Gockel, are about the lives of individual rulers, such as those named "Lord of Time" and "Holder of True Power," and are records of their births, assumptions of power, victories, and deaths.

The spectacular Hieroglyphic Stairway, rediscovered by John Lloyd Stephens overgrown with jungle at the Mayan ruin of Copán, has an inscription on each of its 63 steps, a total of 2500 glyphs. It is considered

Fig. 2.9
An artist's conception of
the way the hieroglyphic
stairway may have looked
when first completed.

one of the wonders of the ancient world. This is the longest Mayan text in existence. Long ago an earthquake jumbled the stairs, and although they have been restored, no one knows for sure if they are in the right order. Archaeologists and Mayan linguists have not been able to read them with any degree of certainty. The glyphs may recount the history of Copán and its rulers, or more likely they record astronomical observations preserved in stone for future calculations.

The Maya had books made from a coated bark paper, but all those from the Classic

Period have disappeared. Paper was made from the bark of the wild fig tree, soaked in water. The inner bark was then peeled away and beaten with stone, mixed with natural gum, and cut into long strips. These paper strips were then coated with lime and dried. The long strips were put together and folded like a screen. They were approximately six metres in length when unfolded. The text was drawn by scribes, who sketched glyphs and figures using colours from vegetables and minerals. Highly decorated wood covers protected the pages of this screen-like book, called a **codex**. In these codices the Maya recorded their history, and it is believed they must have written hundreds of such codices, which they kept in repositories.

Several centuries after the peak of Mayan civilization, in 1561, the last Mayan book repository to survive was put to the torch by the Spanish Franciscan friar, Diego de Landa. Frustrated by the refusal of the Maya to give up their deeply held religious beliefs and practices, he attempted to destroy their religious heritage by confiscating and destroying all Mayan books. He had learned of the existence in the town of Mani of a Mayan book repository, which he ordered publicly burned. His famous description of this event has echoed poignantly down to our time.

> *Among the Maya we found a great number of books written with their characters, and because they contained nothing but superstitions and falsehoods about the devil, we burned them all, which the Indians felt most deeply and over which they showed much sorrow.*

About two million people speak the Maya tongue today, but even they cannot translate most of the picture symbols. Only three Mayan Post-Classic books have survived, the Dresden, Paris, and Madrid Codices, each named for the city in which it is presently located. These books deal with the subjects of religion and astronomy. Much of the Paris Codex is missing, or is so decayed as to be illegible. A fourth codex has been found at the excavations at El Mirador, but the effects over the centuries of water on the pages has cemented them together irreparably.

Spanish chroniclers writing in the period after the conquest reveal the existence of codices dealing with the subjects of science, history, and mythology. The destruction of these codices has severely hampered archaeologists in their attempt to understand the Maya, and has made Mayan studies difficult and problematical. The burning of the Mayan library was a tragic loss of knowledge about this great civilization, as well as an obliteration of the heritage of those Maya and other Amerindians living today.

AGRICULTURE

The Mayan land was especially fertile, and the people were able to build up a large surplus of food. The staple was corn, and most Maya cultivated their own cornfields. They soaked the corn with lime, then ground it with a hand-held stone and formed it into flat, thin cakes. When the ground corn was mixed with red and black kidney beans and toasted, it resembled what we today call a *tortilla*, and when it was

Fig. 2.10
Screen-like folding books called codices filled Mayan repositories. This illustration from the Dresden Codex shows, from left to right, the gods of death, corn, and the north star, each holding the Mayan glyph for corn.

steamed it was like the modern Mexican *tamale.* Other foods, eaten by the Maya, but unknown at that time in Europe, Asia, and Africa, were beans, squash, pumpkin, chili peppers, avocados, sweet potatoes, and tomatoes. Rarely was meat eaten, except at celebrations, where deer or wild boar, hunted late in the Classic Period by bow and arrow, might be served. The Maya drank boiled corn mush and, on rare occasions, wine made from tree bark and honey. Rubber, cotton, and wild fruits were also harvested, and from the cactus plant the Maya made thread for sandals, rope, and cloth. Turkeys, ducks, a stingless bee kept in a hollow log hive, and a bark-less dog used for sacrifice were domesticated.

There were no farm implements such as ploughs, and there were no draught animals to act as beasts of burden. Digging was done with a pointed stick, which was used to turn the soil before sowing the seed. Men and boys would work the fields, hacking away with stone tools at the ever-growing jungle to keep it from overpowering their fields. Possibly they ringed the bark of trees to make the trees dry for burning in areas that were to be farmed later. While the men were working in the cornfields, the women and girls would be at work cooking and weaving.

The Mayan region today is cultivated by a method called **milpa**, involving slashing and burning the jungle growth. Burning the soil, besides clearing it of growth, acts as a form of fertilization by releasing nitrogen and potassium, which provide plant nutrients.

Until recently archaeologists assumed the ancient Maya used the same agricultural technique. But experts questioned how milpa could be the basis of a densely populated urban civilization when this method is only capable of supporting less than 100 people per square kilometre. In the 1950s a University of Pennsylvania archaeological team surveyed the region of the Mayan ceremonial centre at Tikal, the largest of all Mayan cities, and determined that the population had been too dense for slash and burn agriculture to feed it all. Other hypotheses were then suggested to solve the puzzle, including a type of crop rotation that would have allowed for more intensive cultivation, or the widespread planting of the *ramon*, or breadnut tree. These suggestions did not provide satisfactory explanations of how a large population could be sustained.

In the 1970s some startling discoveries

began to provide solutions to the puzzle. On the hillsides near Tikal, archaeologists found the remains of terraces or raised fields, and nearby noticed the remains of an ancient canal system. Modern archaeological techniques, such as aerial photography and radar surveys, showed a canal network spreading over a wide area, with a series of drainage channels crisscrossing the region. A grid of raised fields lay between the channels. Such a system would provide the water necessary for intensive agriculture. Further examination of other Mayan centres showed that practically all were on rivers, swamps, or near lakes. Thus the answer to the puzzle might be that the Mayans had an extensive, well-irrigated **raised field system**, a system that would allow for several seasons of farming in one area. Although this solution is still somewhat controversial, if correct it revolutionizes previously held notions about Mayan population density and subsistence.

One method the Mayan farmer used to preserve the soil from quick exhaustion was to plant several different types of crops in the same field. Even with this method, however, land cleared from jungle growth is usually only fertile for a few seasons, and then must be abandoned to new jungle growth and to insects. Eventually the ability of the soil to grow corn became poorer, and the Mayan farmer would have to move on. Later, when all of the good farmland around a Mayan urban centre became exhausted, the farmer might have to leave the area. This is one possible explanation historians give for the abandonment of so many of their great urban centres. Nevertheless it is worth noting that despite the exhausting cycle of farming and abandoning the land, the Maya still found the time to build the greatest civilization of pre-Columbian America.

RELIGION

Most Maya were farmers, and in most agricultural societies, religion tends to reflect a concern with nature. It is nature, after all, that influences the growth of food. The exact names, number, and hierarchy of all of the many Mayan gods are not known, but it is known that four important gods represented four important forces of nature: rain, thunder, lightning, and hail. Because the planet Venus was so clear in the sky in the morning and evening, mathematical calculations about the seasons, also important to an agricultural people, were based on changes in this planet's position.

There were many other Mayan gods, including gods of death, war, winds, corn, and the north star (a god who watched over travellers). As well, there were goddesses, such as the Goddess of Suicide, an important and respected goddess, as suicide was seen as a positive way to speed the journey to heaven. Of all of the gods and goddesses, the **Chac,** or God of Rain, was undoubtedly the one with which the farmer had the closest and most devoted relationship. This god brought either abundant harvest and thus life, or foul weather, and in its wake, suffering or death.

In surviving codices Chac is shown producing rain by pouring water on the earth from pottery, or by urinating. It was to statues of Chac that the Maya occasionally made human sacrifices during times of drought or other poor crop years, although such human sacrifices were relatively rare and certainly never held the central position in the religion of the Maya that they came to hold in the Aztec religion. People from all over the Mayan realm visited a deep natural well such as the Sacred Cenote (pronounced che-no-tay) at Chichén-Itzá, an underground reservoir where the gods, especially the Rain God, lived. Here victims covered with precious stones and jewels were tossed into the well. Mayan women belonging to important nobles would be thrown into this well at specified times to ask for a good year from the gods for their masters; if they survived the fall, they were hoisted back up by ropes, and would report on life in the underworld.

SACRIFICES

Other choice sacrificial victims were orphans, slaves, virgins, captured enemy warriors, and criminals. The most sought after victims were children, who were often stolen or purchased from nearby towns for a handful of beads each. Animals such as jaguars, dogs, turtles, and turkeys were also sacrificed, in some cases the entire animal, in others just its heart. During the Post-Classic period the incidence of human sacrifice increased markedly under Toltec influence. In recent years the Sacred Cenote at Chichén-Itzá has been plumbed by archaeologists, and many beautiful objects, as well as the bones of sacrificial victims, mostly children, have been raised to the surface.

Two other gods played an important role in the Mayan religion. One was the Supreme God, **Itzamna**, the world creator, a good and kindly god who was given credit for inventing the calendar and glyph writing. This god was very remote from everyday life, and other gods served as intermediaries. Another important god was the feathered serpent **Kulkulkan** (called Quetzalcoatl in *Nahuatl*, the language of the Aztecs), one of the most important of all Mesoamerican figures. This god was a combination "bird-serpent" who had lived among the Maya as a human and had taught them the arts of civilized living. It is possible that this god's life was based upon that of an actual person — a warrior of great ability and courage who later was *deified*, made into a god.

Kulkulkan becomes very important in the subsequent history of the pre-Columbian tribes because of a prophecy he made just before his death. His features are described as blond, unlike those of the dark Amerindian, and just before he died he promised some day to return to lead his people. He also prophesied that, before his return, blond, pale-skinned, bearded men from the sea would conquer the people. He did not die, but disappeared from the earth or in some versions was consumed by fire.

Mayan society was in effect a **theocracy**; Mayan priests played an important role in the lives of the people. These priests were called *Itzas*, after Itzamna, the long-nosed supreme god. The Itzas formed a ruling class of leaders in politics, culture, and religion. The priests studied the movements of the heavenly bodies and invented the calendar. They were the ones who knew and could predict the nature and moods of the gods. A child's life was predetermined by the priest's study of the heavens at the day

Itzamna, head of the Maya pantheon.

Kukulcan, the wind god.

Chac, the rain god.

The god of sacrifice

Fig. 2.11
Mayan gods.

and hour of its birth. Many rituals were celebrated throughout the child's life at times predetermined by these priests, including flattening the forehead and celebrating puberty and marriage.

During times of great natural disaster such as hurricanes or droughts, the Itzas would lead the human sacrifice in order to appease the angry gods. The usual method of sacrifice was to lead a victim, who had been painted blue, up the steps of a pyramid. Here the victim would be stretched over a stone, and while elderly men called *chacs* held the arms and legs of the victim, the priest cut out the heart with an obsidian blade. The idols of the gods were then anointed with the victim's blood and the corpse was flung down the temple steps. Here a waiting priest would flay its skin and dance in it while the spectators ate the remains, except for the hands and feet, which were saved for the priests. Other forms of sacrifice included the "arrow sacrifice" — filling up the chest of a victim with arrows; decapitation, hanging, drowning, and mutilation.

Fig. 2.12
The Mayan Sacred
Ball Court at Copán.

In the Mayan religion earth had been created and destroyed many times. The world was a flat space, with a huge tree in the centre and smaller trees at the four corners of the surface, in between thirteen heavens and nine underworlds. This world was carried on the back of a giant crocodile floating in a lily pond.

It is probable that ordinary Mayans understood little about the deeper aspects of their religion, which they left to the priesthood. Their participation in religion took the form of involvement in ceremonies, dancing, singing, fasting, drinking alcoholic beverages, and ritual bloodletting by piercing their ears, nose, lips, tongue, and sexual organs with obsidian blades or stingray spines.

THE SACRED BALL GAME

All aspects of Mayan life were affected by religion, even sport. The Maya had a favourite ball game called *pok-a-tok*, which was played within a walled-in field about the size of two tennis courts, with a stone ring at each end set vertically some ten metres high on the wall. This game, probably first played by the Olmecs around 500 B.C.E., combined recreation with religious rituals of death and sacrifice, and with complex astronomical symbolism. The movement of the ball possibly depicted the perpetual movement of the sun throughout the year, the stone rings representing the spring and autumn equinoxes.

Although scholars are not absolutely certain how the game was played, they have been able to piece together some details from surviving illustrations in pottery and stone. The game was a kind of cross between soccer, volleyball, and basketball, and could be played by two people or two teams. Players had to be in excellent physical condition, as the play was non-stop. The use of a rubber ball in the game was probably the first use of rubber in history. The object of the game was to keep the ball from touching the ground and eventually to push it across an endline. A player could only touch the ball with the hips, knees, and elbows, but not with the hands or feet. The ball could be bounced on the playing surface and off the walls. Because of the hardness of the ball, players wore thick leather and wood padding on their hips and knees, as well as face masks. Despite these precautions, there were many injuries and sometimes fatalities during a game.

Spectators sat on stone bleachers set above the walls. There seems to have been much gambling on the game, with spectators wagering jewelry, property, slaves, and sometimes themselves as slaves. In some cases, if a player scored a goal through the vertical ring, he could demand all the jewelry and even the clothing of the spectators. If such a goal was scored, the spectators understandably would make a dash for the exits, but few goals ever were scored through the narrow ring, set vertically ten metres high on the wall. Important political and religious leaders attended games before important battles, and each game concluded with a religious ceremony. In some cases the losers were sacrificed, and a rock carving from Chichén-Itzá shows ball players being decapitated.

MAYAN CITIES

As we have seen, earlier archaeologists could not explain how a large population could survive on slash and burn milpas, and so they assumed Mayan population density was low. They thought that Classic period sites such as Tikal and Copán were ceremonial centres rather than cities. This view of these population centres is changing as a result of the new findings about Mayan agriculture. In addition, archaeological evidence is now making it clear that larger Mayan centres contained administrative and residential buildings, rather than just temples and religious sites, in order to meet the needs of an urban populace. Now we can explain how a larger population subsisted and can probably be safe in referring to Mayan centres as cities.

Mayan cities contained a central core of ceremonial and administrative buildings and centralized markets, tapering off into suburbs of huts made of daub-and-wattle (mud and clay plastered over interlaced twigs). Commercial activity mainly consisted of trade with other centres or with non-Mayan peoples. This trade was a vital factor in unifying the far-flung area where Mayan culture predominated. Most trade was by barter (goods traded for goods), but the cacao bean was used as currency when needed. This bean was scarce, and spoiled quickly, making it difficult to hoard — both excellent qualities for currency. Hot chocolate was a popular drink among the nobility, who liked to show off their wealth by, in effect, drinking money.

Although many Mayan Classic Period cities were linked through trade and royal marriages, each was basically independent, and none ruled over others. Within the cities there was a clearly defined class system dominated by a wealthy, *hereditary* elite that held considerable power, owned the land, carried on the trade, and filled the priesthood. Everyone else was of the lower class, many of them held in servitude.

While few Maya actually lived within the ceremonial centre core, most lived just outside. The jungle growth was too thick to move too far into the interior. It is also probable that it was very hard for these deeply religious people to live too far removed from the temples. Mayan city centres were the focus of the religious rituals that gave value and meaning to the life of the average citizen. For these devout people religion was centred around the main temple built atop a huge stone pyramid in the heart of each centre, and surrounded by several courtyards.

Many of these pyramids and temples were great architectural achievements, beautifully and painstakingly built by hand from stone. The more important temples were placed on the top of pyramids and capped by decorative designs. These were probably brightly painted, and were decorated with sculptures cut into the stone or made from stucco and added on. By comparison, the interiors were nearly bare, containing several small, narrow cells, usually very damp and covered by white plaster. A few temples interiors have been found with glyphs, murals, and even graffiti. These

urban areas and their great stone temples survived long after Mayan civilization collapsed.

It remains a mystery how the Maya actually built such solidly crafted stone cities, particularly since they had to move boulders of many tonnes without wheeled vehicles, metal tools, or beasts of burden. It remains a mystery as well how the Maya carved deeply into the stone with only simple stone tools. The amount of labour expended in hauling and carving must have been phenomenal. There is no mystery as to why the Maya did not have the wheel. Pushing a wheeled vehicle through a jungle or forest is not a productive activity. And there were no draught animals to pull such a vehicle. Yet the Maya understood the use of the wheel, because children's toys with wheels have been found.

Within the urban centres the Maya had an excellent network of raised roads built of large stones covered by rubble and surfaced with a form of cement. These roads were sometimes nearly ten metres wide, and formed broad avenues connecting important ceremonial centres. Just outside the circle of streets and buildings of the ceremonial centre were narrow roads. Along these roads were small, oval-shaped homes with palm-thatched roofs. The single room was divided by a high partition into two quarters, one for sleeping and one for domestic activities. These homes were made from reeds or cane, and had earth and stone floors to allow for drainage. At intervals along the streets were other buildings that were used for cooking and storage. Inside the home were wood stools and benches, pottery, baskets, and stone tools. Beds were

Fig. 2.13
Mayan corbelled arch
at the Governor's
Palace, Uxmal,
Yucatán.

made from fibre matting hung between two poles.

Each urban centre had its own sacred ball court, and some of the larger cities had rainwater reservoirs, sweat baths used for medicinal purposes, and astronomical observatories. Immediately outside the city were the milpas.

Nearly thirty sizeable Mayan cities have been excavated, and about one hundred smaller sites have also been examined by archaeologists. Some of these cities astound modern viewers by their beauty and scope. In the dense jungles of southern Mexico, Guatemala, Honduras, northern El Salvador, and Belize, amidst the noise of howling monkeys and the menace of poisonous snakes, lie the ruins of hundreds of smaller Mayan settlements, waiting to be discovered and excavated by adventurous archaeologists.

In the last ten years important excavations have been made at a site called *El Mirador*, once a Mayan centre of perhaps 80 000 people, and considered the most important discovery since the time of Stephens and Catherwood in the nineteenth century. This site still has many ridges and mounds under the jungle floor, which seem to indicate the presence of homes, temples, and pyramids, some as large as a modern city block.

In archaeology, assumptions made in the past often have to be reassessed in the light of new findings. The findings at El Mirador are an example of such a reassessment. For example, pottery discovered at El Mirador dates from 400 B.C.E., which may indicate that Mayan civilization lasted up to 1500 years, some six centuries longer than had previously been believed. Also, the Maya have always been thought of as a non-military society, but findings at this site show huge walls with structures at the top that some authorities believe may have been lookout towers or turrets, both of which are used for military defense.

The genius of Mayan architecture also extended to the arch. The Maya used a **corbelled arch** such as the one pictured here.

Fig. 2.14
This Mayan noble with folded arms is considered a masterpiece of the woodworker's art.

These arches are formed by placing stone blocks in a step pattern and linking them with extremely strong mortar. Because the walls had to carry the load supported by this type of arch, Mayan walls had to be very thick, at times much thicker than the actual space of the room. The Maya also learned to make stucco and mortar, and developed the technique of building each new building on the foundation of the last so that space was not wasted.

MAYAN ART

Most Mayan art during the Classic Period depicted religious themes or ruling dynasties. Important cities had their own recognizable artistic styles, especially in the most beautiful Mayan art forms: sculpture and ceramics. Mayan art often shows haughty noble persons in situations designed to enhance their status as rulers, frequently displaying them in full regalia seated on thrones, or carried by attendants on litters, covered in jewels, receiving slaves or tributes, and holding symbols of authority.

The Maya were also fine craftsmen in weaving and featherwork, jadework, basket weaving, and leatherwork, and especially in shell, bone, and wood sculpting. They often used their finest work to decorate their temples. Most examples of these crafts have rotted over time from the humidity of the jungle region, but a few wood pieces have been preserved . These are considered masterful works of the woodcutter's art. Jade, being the most sought after stone, is often found in tombs of the nobility, buried with the dead as offerings, and worn by the corpse in beautiful crowns, necklaces, bracelets, earplugs, and rings. Frequently a single jade bead was placed in the mouth of the dead person to provide for the purchase of food in the next life. Mayan upper classes were known to set jade into their teeth as a sign of status.

As in the building of Mayan cities, everything about Mayan art indicates that a gargantuan amount of energy must have been expended to glorify religion. The workers or commoners who expended the labour are not shown. Although most Mayan art has been lost, there still could be some beautiful Mayan works of art preserved in some buried Mayan city today. Such thoughts motivate the archaeologist.

One of the scandals of our modern period is the looting of many unexplored Mayan sites. Looting occurs when wealthy collectors are prepared to pay for stolen artifacts from these looted sites; the artifacts are often damaged beyond archaeological usefulness by the looter. Looting means that much information is lost forever, and the heritage of a people is destroyed. In recent years many countries have agreed to enforce laws against smuggling artifacts, but the practice still goes on.

MAYAN RITES OF PASSAGE

Little is known about everyday Mayan life because few artifacts relating to Maya commoners have survived. What we do know comes mostly from the testimony of Spanish chroniclers who observed Mayan activity long after the end of the Classic Period.

The birth of a child was considered a mark of approval by the gods, and thus was a very important event in Mayan life. Priests named the child and predicted its future by horoscope as an aid to the parents in its upbringing. Mayan children were made more beautiful by having their foreheads flattened and their eyes crossed, and older children had their earlobes, lips, and one nostril pierced for jewelry. Girls wore a red shell dangling from a string about their waist until a puberty ceremony at age twelve; its removal signalled that the girl was eligible for marriage.

Marriages were normally arranged by the parents. The father of an eighteen-year-old boy would make arrangements with the father of the girl through a matchmaker. Young women who were well trained in domestic activities like cooking and sewing were most sought after. Girls were expected to observe the long-established customs of Mayan society, such as lowering the eyes, turning the back, and stepping aside when passing a man. Girls were held to an ideal of chastity, and were whipped, and their wounds rubbed with pepper, if they strayed from this ideal.

Wealthier men could afford many wives, but a commoner could usually support only one. A husband lived with the wife's family for several years, working with his father-in-law while he proved his worth. Wives rarely talked to or dined with their husbands, and only danced with them at special festivals. Divorce was very common; marriages could be dissolved at any time merely by mutual agreement. Adultery on the part of the wife could be punished by dropping a large stone from a great height on her lover's head.

The Maya thought that sickness was the mark of the gods' displeasure. A priest would be called to prescribe rituals and potions. Potions were often made from such items as blood, bat wings, ground iguana, crocodile teeth, worms, animal excrement, or herbs. The Maya looked to death with trepidation and yet with the hope that they might spend eternity among the thirteen heavens. A Maya could ensure this by committing suicide, being killed in battle, or dying during childbirth or as a sacrifice, thereby avoiding an underworld of cold and hunger. Most peasants were buried under the floor of their houses, which were then abandoned. Bodies were encased in cotton, and pottery, corn, and other property were buried with the deceased to support them in the coming journey.

THE DECLINE AND FALL OF THE MAYA

More than a century after the rediscovery of the ruins of Mayan cities by Stephens and Catherwood, the cause or causes of the collapse of Classic Mayan civilization remains a mystery. The dates on smashed stelae show that urban centre after urban centre was abandoned sometime between the period beginning just before the ninth century to just after the tenth century C.E. Temples and other buildings were left in mid-construction, ruling dynasties came to an end, and artistic, religious, and intellectual life declined everywhere. No new stelae were constructed, a final sign of decline for a people who had been so dedicated to recording their history on these slab monuments. The jungle reclaimed Mayan cities seemingly at the height of their achievements.

There has been much speculation, but no hard evidence, about the collapse. Some of the causes put forward include the catastrophic impact of climatic change, famine, conquest by invading armies, earthquakes, plagues, and even a revolt against the priesthood and ruling dynasties.

It is possible that the Mayan population

Fig. 2.15
An artist's conception of the main temple of Chichén-Itzá as it may have looked at its peak.

may have become too large for the food supply to support, with resulting hunger and even starvation. Poor and wasteful agricultural methods may eventually have led to what one author has called "agricultural exhaustion." Skeletons from Mayan graves of this period are small in size compared with earlier skeletons, and there is evidence of scurvy, periodontal disease, and rickets, all of which result from malnutrition. Some experts have speculated that commoners may have rebelled against priests and rulers who were hoarding food for themselves.

There is no archaeological evidence that hostile armies invaded Mayan cities at this time, although in one region, the Yucatán, a warlike people called the Toltecs from central Mexico somehow combined with the Maya to produce a hybrid Maya-Toltec culture. There is also no convincing archaeological proof of widespread plague or natural disaster such as earthquake or drought, yet these possibilities cannot be completely ruled out. If Mayan society were already weakening, the scale of disease, invasion, or natural disaster would not have to be great to bring about a collapse.

Some authorities speculate that an

increasingly acquisitive and militaristic Mayan society may have begun to fight among its own city states. Such fighting inevitably causes a decline in trade, which may have led to a greater gap than before in living standards between rich and the poor. The Mayan nobility may have grown more and more insistent on underfed peasants labouring to build monumental religious buildings and palaces, and this could have led to revolution. About this time the Mayan peasants may have learned to use the bow and arrow from nearby peoples, and this may have aided them immeasurably in any rebellion against the elite. In city state after city state the rulers and the priesthood may have been toppled and killed, leading to an end of the learned classes who held the key to civilization. In the view of one Mayanist, the death rate increased among two groups vital to keeping population stable: infants and young women, leading to a decline in the population.

However, one corner of the Mayan world did manage to survive and thrive for a time in northern Yucatán and Belize, where the Post-Classic city of Chichén-Itzá flourished after the abandonment of the Classic Mayan cities. At this site there is evidence that the indigenous Maya associated with a group of people called the Toltecs from highland Mexico, the most powerful people in Mesoamerica about 1000 C.E.

The nature of this association is unclear. Experts are uncertain whether it represents a conquest by the Toltecs, possibly in 987 C.E., or even earlier, possibly in the mid-seventh century. Or it may have been a peaceful assimilation with the far superior Mayan culture. Scenes found at Chichén-Itzá of battles and of Mayan prisoners being sacrificed lead some archaeologists to conclude that the invaders conquered the Mayan population militarily, but this evidence is not conclusive. In any case, there was a vigourous revival of Mayan civilization with Chichén-Itzá as the cultural and economic centre. This Mayan civilization was much more warlike and had a greater obsession with human sacrifice than before.

The nature and causes of the combining of Mayan and Toltec culture remain one of the most difficult problems in Mayan archaeology. Even this Mayan-Toltec centre, alas, was abandoned sometime before 1224 C.E.

By the time Spanish ships arrived off the coast of the Yucatán peninsula, the Classic period of Mayan civilization had long been over, and Chichén-Itzá was in ruins. The fringes of the Mayan realm were under the control of a more warlike and less civilized people, the Aztecs of the central valley of Mexico, whom you will read about in the next chapter. The Maya living outside of the Aztec empire traded with these rulers of Mexico, who had little knowledge of the great Mayan cultural heritage.

In the period between the abandonment of Chichén-Itzá and other Mayan-Toltec centres and the arrival of the Spaniards, Mayan economic and military activity was centered at *Mayapán* on the Yucatán peninsula. Here the surviving Maya hired fierce Mexican mercenary soldiers to defend the city behind stone walls. Excavations at Mayapán show a decay in the quality and beauty of art and architecture. The few religious buildings are small and poorly built, probably reflecting a decline in the role of religion and priests in the life of the people.

Mayapán was in constant conflict with other cities in the Yucatán, and around 1441 C.E. was sacked and burned. The survivors of the destruction of Mayapán abandoned that location to establish new settlements, and by the end of the fifteenth century Yucatán had sixteen separate feuding provinces, each with its own army. Warfare was frequent, often over boundary disputes or for the purpose of obtaining victims for sacrifice.

THE MAYA AFTER THE ARRIVAL OF THE SPANIARDS

To this rise of militarism and decline in the artistic, economic, political, and intellectual life was added a series of natural disasters. A hurricane did untold damage about 1464, and a pestilence followed in 1481. Locusts later attacked crops in the Yucatán, destroying agriculture there for five years. In 1514 the smallpox virus spread from the Spaniards in Panama to the Maya, causing terrible suffering among its victims.

The Spaniards were quick to exploit the problems of the Maya. Most Spanish colonists knew practically nothing and cared less for the past achievements of Mayan civilization. Seeking land and cheap labour, they saw the Maya as devil worshippers, and began to confiscate their lands and obliterate their religion and culture. The Maya were forcibly moved from their towns to areas under Spanish control, where they could work under Spanish supervision.

Temples and idols were smashed, pagan rituals forbidden, and the wearing of ceremonial costumes banned. All Maya were taught Christianity, and any violations of the new faith were brutally punished. Despite the attempts of some missionaries to protect them, the Maya were tortured: they were scalded with boiling water, their joints were stretched with pulleys, and they were mutilated, whipped, and beaten.

In the face of these conditions the Maya periodically rose up against their Spanish oppressors, massacred the colonists and their livestock, and destroyed their towns and crops. These were rebellions of frustration, however, without the organization or technology necessary to obtain a lasting victory. As the decades passed the Mayan cultural heritage faded from the memory of the descendents of these once great people, and the understanding of glyphs and the calendar was completely lost. Ironically it was the Franciscan friar Diego de Landa, destroyer of the Mayan book repository, who salvaged what remained of the knowledge of Mayan culture.

Landa, in his zeal to convert what he saw as heathen Amerindians, immersed himself in Mayan language and culture. He lived with surviving Mayan nobles, and laboriously gathered and recorded information about Mayan customs in his extensive travels. The result was a book entitled *Relacion de las Cosas de Yucatán*, easily the most thorough and complete study of the Maya in the period of Spanish rule. Landa's book remains a revealing source about Mayan customs, arts, ceremonies, religious practices, calendrics, and especially Mayan glyphs.

Fig. 2.16
From the mural of Bonampak, this scene shows captives being tortured in various ways. One captive has had his nails pulled out, the decapitated head of another and a corpse lie nearby, another appears to be begging the Mayan soldier for his life.

THE MAYA TODAY

The Maya are not a vanished race; over two million descendants of the ancient Maya live in Mexico and Central America today. Here they combine such modern developments as public schools, stores, movies, motorized transport and the many uses of gasoline, machetes, and household appliances with their traditional ways. They still live in stone homes with thatched roofs, built without nails, much like those of their ancestors. They wear sandals made from vegetable fibre and animal hides, and the women still grind corn into dough for *tortillas* by using round stones called *metates*. Farming methods have changed little over the intervening centuries; corn, beans, and other crops are still planted in milpas by farmers using pointed sticks to dig the soil. In some areas traditional Mayan clothing is still worn. The Christian religion of these people is a mixture of modern Christianity and traditional Mayan practices; local Christian saints very much resemble former pagan gods. The Maya still leave offerings and chant prayers to traditional gods during childbirth and marriage ceremonies and when crops are planted.

One group of Maya, a remote forest tribe called the Lacandon, adhere closely to some of the traditions of their ancestors. They use traditional methods to weave cloth and make pottery in small groups. They live in thatched homes and carry on age-old religious rituals and ceremonies. After the Spaniards failed to Christianize them, they had been forgotten by the rest of the world until the middle of this century, when the resources of their region, mahogany, oil, and chicle, used in the making of gum, brought in prospectors. These newcomers also brought diseases, and the population of the Lacandon dropped to about 200 people before modern medicine saved the remnant.

In the winter of 1945 a documentary film maker noticed that Lacandon men made pilgrimages to a secret location in a ruin near their settlement. In exchange for shotguns, ammunition, and cash, he convinced them to reveal their shrine, and became the first non-Maya to see fabulous Classic Period paintings on the walls of a small chamber of the ruin. This site, *Bonampak*, Mayan for "painted walls," turned out to be one of the greatest discoveries in the history of Mesoamerican archaeology. The paintings consisted of three murals, which depicted the story of a battle and its aftermath and victory celebrations, and showed scenes of priests, nobles, armies, captives, dancers, musicians, human sacrifices, and much more. Realistic scenes of torture, severed heads, sacrifices, and Mayan ladies drawing blood from their tongues, all in vivid colours, have been a key factor in reassessing the level of violence in the Classic Period. In addition, these murals, dated by inscriptions at around 750 to 800 C.E., present a wealth of information on Classic period Maya and the way they actually looked, lived, and behaved, the clothing they wore, the rituals they performed, their methods of warfare, and many of their everyday activities.

No doubt the enigmas and unanswered questions about the ancient Maya will continue to intrigue scholars and students for a long time to come, although new excavations and improved methods of analyzing data lead to new findings and breakthroughs every year. The mystery of the collapse of a great civilization presents a challenge to our understanding of the forces that shape and act upon all societies.

HIGHLIGHTS

1. The Maya of the Classic Period (about 300 to 900 C.E.) had the most advanced civilization of pre-Columbian America. Their achievements in such fields as astronomy, architecture, hieroglyph writing, and mathematics far surpassed those of their contemporaries in Europe during the Dark Ages.

2. An American amateur archaeologist named John Lloyd Stephens and his companion, artist Frederick Catherwood, helped to reawaken interest in the Maya in the nineteenth century. They did this by travelling from 1839 onwards to some 44 forgotten Mayan cities overgrown by jungle, and by publishing lavishly illustrated and popular books based on their adventures.

3. The Mayan people mastered the ability

to produce large surpluses of food through agriculture before other tribes of the Americas did. This gave them the leisure time to be able to develop science, writing, and the finer arts; they developed a culture greatly influenced by the earlier Olmec culture.

4. The Maya entered upon a great period of achievement known as the Classic Period sometime in the fourth century C.E. This Classic Period saw the building of great pyramids and temples, thriving cities, and a widespread cultural area based on trade.

5. The Maya, being a primarily agricultural people, depended a great deal on knowledge of the seasons and the ability to predict climate patterns. They saw time as cyclical, with events repeating themselves. In order to understand and predict the forces of time, they developed a remarkably accurate calendar, more accurate than any found elsewhere in the world until several centuries later.

6. The Maya developed a very advanced system of writing that enabled them to convey ideas through symbols known as glyphs. It has been a slow process for experts to decode the symbols, as no key to them has been found. As we translate more and more of them, our knowledge of the Maya deepens, and many old ideas have to be discarded or revised.

7. The Maya recorded their history on upright slabs called stelae. From what has been decoded by translating the glyphs from surviving stelae, we have learned a great deal about Mayan history, but much is still undecipherable.

8. The Maya had an extensive library that was burned by zealous Spanish missionaries, causing the people great grief. Only three books survive, on the subjects of astronomy and religion.

9. The Mayan number system was far more flexible and easier to use than any other found in the world to that time, including those developed in Greece or Rome. It was a vigesimal system, based on units of twenty, needing only three symbols, a dot , a bar, and a shell. The shell stood for zero, an advanced mathematical concept.

10. The Mayan urban and religious centres and stone pyramids and temples were great architectural achievements, although it remains a mystery how great boulders were moved long distances without the use of beasts of burden or the wheel. It is also a mystery how elaborate carvings were cut deeply into the stone without the use of metal tools. The knowledge of how this was done has been lost, even to the descendants of the Maya living today.

11. By the time of the arrival of the Spanish conquerors in the fifteenth century, the once great Mayan people had been reduced from a complex to a simple way of life, the secrets of their civilization long forgotten by their descendants.

12. Without any direct evidence, experts can only speculate about the reasons why Mayan city after Mayan city was abandoned sometime between the ninth and tenth centuries. Explanations offered range from natural disaster to foreign invasion to internal weak-

nesses leading to revolution. One centre did manage to thrive for another few centuries, in the Yucatán, but it too was abandoned for unknown reasons in the thirteenth century.

13. In the period after the end of the Classic and Post-Classic periods of Mayan history, the craftsmanship and art of the Maya degenerated. By the time of the arrival of the Spaniards, the surviving Mayan cities were severely disunited, a situation exploited by the Spanish conquerors. Seeking cheap labour and land, they ruthlessly supressed the remaining features of Mayan culture in order to force the Maya to work under their supervision. In time virtually all the secrets of Mayan culture, including the meaning of Mayan glyphs, were forgotten.

TERMS TO UNDERSTAND

Write a one-sentence explanation of each of the following terms. Write a sentence using each term.

codex
corbelled arch
glyphs
Itzas
katun
Kulkulkan
milpa
raised field system of agriculture
theocracy
stelae
vigesimal

DEVELOPING CRITICAL THINKING SKILLS ABOUT CONCEPTS IN THE SOCIAL SCIENCES.
FOR INDIVIDUAL OR GROUP PRESENTATION.

1. *COMPARATIVE STUDIES*: Define how the following concepts applied to Mayan society: civilization, society, culture, economics, technology, sex roles, politics, values, and leadership. Compare the Mayan applications of these concepts with another civilization at a different time in history.

2. *CULTURE SHOCK*: What is meant by the term "culture shock"? How did it affect both the Maya and the Spanish when they first came in contact with each other at the end of the fifteenth century?

   Can you think of other examples of culture shock in history? Have you ever experienced it? When and where?

3. *ECONOMICS*: Why was agriculture the most common form of economic activity in the Mayan realm? What was the relationship between improvements in agriculture, the development of religion, and the growth of Mayan cities?

4. *CENSORSHIP*: Why do you think the Spanish missionaries burned Mayan writings in the sixteenth century? Why did the Maya react with such anguish? In your opinion can there ever be a justification for destroying a book? Explain.

   Book burning has not been unknown in the twentieth century. Research the Nazi burnings of books following their takeover in Germany in the 1930s.

5. *POPULARIZING HISTORY*: What do you think made the books by Stephens and Catherwood so popular in their day, with people who had never heard of the Maya and their civilization? Are there any such books in recent history about exotic subjects that have been best-sellers? In your opinion, what has made these books popular?

6. *ETHNOCENTRISM*: Some of the Mayan ideas of attractiveness seem strange, even bizarre to us, such as the flattened foreheads and the crossed eyes. Are there any of our ideas of what is attractive and appealing that future civilizations may find strange or even bizarre? Give examples. Role play a situation where an archaeologist from the future describes some customs in a modern high school.

7. *SPORT*: The Maya were not the first or last civilization in which sport had an important part to play in the political and religious life of the people. It has been said that the role of sports in our society is more important than merely entertainment. What do you think is meant by this statement? Cite examples where sport today has more than just recreational meaning for people. What are the symbolic roles of athletes and athletic contests?

8. *DEVELOPING HYPOTHESES*: There is much about Mayan civilization that remains a mystery. Often archaeologists begin a search for answers with inferences or speculations. Speculate about the following:
   a) How did the Maya move great stone boulders over long distances without the use of beasts of burden or the wheel?
   b) Why did the Maya not use the wheel for labour when they knew and understood its use, as proven by wheeled children's toys?
   c) How did the Maya carve deeply into rocks without metal tools?
   d) It remains a mystery why the Mayan civilization fell. Looking at our civilization today, what factors could cause it to fall some day? Can any of these factors have been present in Mayan history?

RELATED TOPICS FOR RESEARCH AND PRESENTATION

The travels of Stephens and Catherwood
How the Maya calendar works
The astronomy of the ancient Maya
Mayan glyphs
Mayan religion
Tikal
Copán
El Mirador
Palenque
The murals of Bonampak
Uxmal
The Toltecs
Chichén-Itzá
The looting of archaeological sites
The Maya today

FOR ADDITIONAL READING AND RESEARCH

MAGAZINE AND JOURNAL ARTICLES

Note: the December 1975 National Geographic magazine has four excellent articles on

the Maya; these would be a good introduction for the interested student. The articles are as follows:

"Children of Time," Howard LaFay

"Resurrecting the Grandeur of Tikal," William Coe

"Riddle of the Glyphs," George E. Stuart

"A Traveler's Tale of Ancient Tikal," Alice J. Hall

see National Geographic also for:

"Column," W. E. Garrett, May 1987

"The Oldest Known Maya," Norman Hammond, July, 1982

Articles of interest from other journals are:

"Ancient Maya Tomb Discovered," J. Greenberg. *Science News*, May 26, 1984.

"Ancient Mayan Calendar Discovered to be Genius," *Astronomy*, July, 1983.

"Blood and Sacrifice," B. Bower. *Science News*, June 7, 1986.

"Buried Treasure in the Jungle," *Time Magazine*, June 4, 1984.

"Cache Withdrawal at Ancient Maya Site," B. Bower. *Science News*, April 4, 1987.

"The Caracol Tower at Chichén-Itzá: An Ancient Astronomical Observatory," Aveni, A., and others. *Science Magazine*, Volume 188, June 6, 1975.

"City of Kings and Commoners, Copán," G.E. Stuart. *National Geographic*, October, 1989.

"The Constant Bloodbath of the Antique World," *The Economist*, February 14, 1987.

"Copán, A Royal Maya Tomb Discovered," Richard A. Fasquelle and William L. Fast. *National Geographic*, October, 1989.

"Dig It, (Remains of Woman Discovered in Belize Tomb)," *Ms.*, August, 1988.

"The Emergence of Mayan Civilization," N. Hammond. *Scientific American*, August, 1986.

"Lamanai, Belize: Summary of Excavation Results," 1974-1980, *Journal of Field Archaeology*, Volume 8, 1980.

"La Ruta Maya," Wilbur E. Garrett. *National Geographic*, October, 1989.

"Late Maya Culture Gets an Island Lift," B. Bower. *Science News*, July 8, 1989.

"The Lost Language of Coba," V. Morell. *Science*, March 1986.

"Maya Writing," D. Stuart and S.D. Houston. *Scientific American*, August, 1989.

"A Mayan Revelation," (Bonampak), S. Sesin. *World Press Review*, October, 1988.

"Satellites Help in Study of Ancient Civilization," *Astronomy*, August, 1987.

"Tracking the Maya After Classic Crash," *Science News*, September 10, 1988.

"Treasures of the Guatemala Rain Forest," A. Wade. *The New Leader*, April 3-17, 1989.

"Unravelling Another Mayan Mystery," A. Chen. *Discover Magazine*, June, 1987.

"What can 411 Maya do in 100 days?," (Copán) Elliot Abrams. *Discover Magazine*, March 1988.

"Why Were the Aztecs and Mayas Stuck in the Stone Age? Obsidian, a Kind of Volcanic Glass May Be the Answer," T. Stucker. *Earth Science Magazine*, Summer, 1987.

"New Clues to the Mayan Mystery," N, Angier. *Discover Magazine*, June, 1981.

BOOKS

Benson, Elizabeth P., *The Maya World*. Thomas Crowell, New York, 1977.

Bernal, Ignacio, *Mexico Before Cortez*. Dolphin Books, Garden City, New York, 1963.

Coe, Michael, D., *The Maya*. Thames and Hudson, London, third edition, 1984.

———, *The Maya Scribe and His World*. Grolier, New York, 1973.

Culbert, Patrick T., ed., *The Classic Maya Collapse*. University of New Mexico Press, Albuquerque, 1977.

Gallenkamp, Charles, *Maya: The Riddle and Rediscovery of a Lost Civilization*. Third revised edition. David McKay, New York, 1985.

Gallenkamp, Charles and Regina Elise Johnson, eds., *Maya, Treasures of an Ancient Civilization.* Harry N. Abrams, New York, 1985.

Hammond, Norman, *Ancient Maya Civilization.* Rutgers Univ. Press, New Brunswick, New Jersey, 1982.

Henderson, John S., *The World of the Ancient Maya.* Cornell University Press, Ithaca, New York, 1981.

Ivanoff, Pierre, *Maya.* Grosset & Dunlop, New York, 1973.

Morris, Walter F., *Living Maya.* Abrams, 1987.

Muser, Curt, *Facts and Artifacts of Ancient America.* E. P. Dutton, New York, 1978.

Pendergast, David M., *Excavations at Altun Ha, Belize, 1964-1970. Volumes 1 & 2.* Royal Ontario Museum, Toronto, 1982.

Proskouriakoff, Tatiana, *An Album of Maya Architecture.* University of Oklahoma Press, Norman, Oklahoma, 1963.

Schele, Linda & Mary Ellen Miller, *The Blood of Kings: Dynasty and Ritual in Maya Art.* George Braziller. Kimbell Art Museum, Ft. Worth, Texas, 1986.

Stephens, John L., *Incidents of Travel in Central America, Chiapas, and Yucatán.* 2 volumes, New York, 1841.

Stephens, John L., *Incidents of Travel in Yucatán.* 2 volumes, New York, 1843.

Stuart, Gene S. and Stuart, George E., *The Mysterious Maya.* National Geographic Society, Washington, D. C., 1977.

Thompson, J. Eric, *The Rise and Fall of Maya Civilization.* University of Oklahoma Press, Norman, Oklahoma, 1976.

Tompkins, Peter, *Mysteries of the Mexican Pyramids.* Harper and Row, New York, 1976.

Turner, Wilson G., *Maya Designs.* Dover Publications, New York, 1980.

Wauchope, Robert, *Lost Tribes & Sunken Continents: Myth and Method in the Study of American Indians.* The University of Chicago Press, Chicago, Illinois, 1962.

Willey, Gordon R., and Sabloff, Jeremy A., *PreColumbian Archaeology.* Scientific American, W. H. Freeman, San Francisco, California, 1979.

Wright, Ronald, *Time Among The Mayas.* Viking Press, Toronto, 1989.

CHAPTER THREE

THE AZTECS

The Aztecs were an obscure northern tribe that entered the central valley of Mexico late in the pre-Columbian period and rose to dominance in the century before the arrival of Columbus. Their culture was based on a religion that required constant sacrifice of human blood to feed its gods. Aztec domination was ended by the invasion of Hernan Cortés and a few hundred Spanish conquistadores in 1519. The story of the Aztecs and their culture, and their destruction by the Spaniards, is one of the most gripping of all historical epics.

INTRODUCTION

Sometime near the beginning of the fourteenth century C.E. a hitherto unimportant people migrated southwards into the valley of Mexico. These people were not allowed by the valley tribes to settle on the already crowded land, and ended up having to live on a small island in the midst of a snake-infested swampland. Out of such humble beginnings arose a great city, the focal point of a civilization that occupied the centre stage of the history of the Mexican valley for nearly two centuries before the Spanish conquest. These were the Mexica (pronounced Me-*shi*-ca); we call them the Aztecs, an alternative name for them derived from Azatlan, a region of Mexico from which they claimed to come.

During the era of their domination the Aztecs forced surrounding peoples and tribes to pay huge amounts of tribute in food, precious stones, and slaves, and to supply victims for human sacrifice. They gained a reputation for unprecedented bloodthirstiness, their gods demanding large quantities of human blood and the hearts of captive warriors.

The Aztecs were able to dominate the huge region from the Pacific to the Gulf Coast and well to the south through their cruel and brutal tactics, but they did not obtain loyalty from those they conquered.

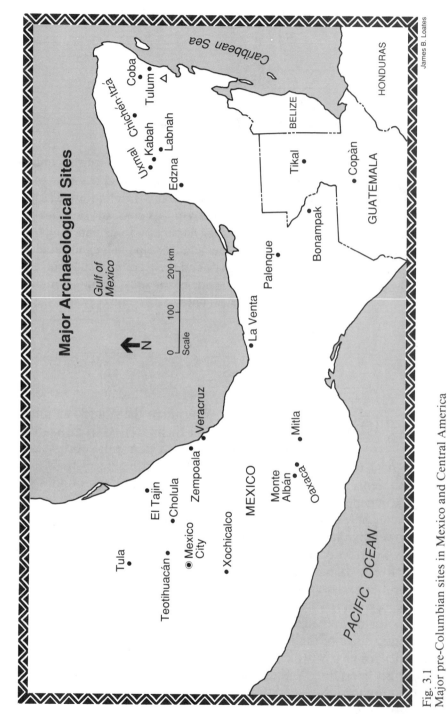

Fig. 3.1
Major pre-Columbian sites in Mexico and Central America

Thus, when the Spaniards invaded after 1519, the Aztec empire quickly crumbled; the Aztec people were overcome by a mere handful of invaders who were able to find allies among the people the Aztecs had subdued. Aztec culture then quickly disappeared from history.

PART ONE: THE AZTEC EMPIRE

ORIGINS

According to their own legends, the Aztecs left the home of their ancestors in approximately the year 1168 C.E. and migrated southwards. This journey lasted a century and a half. Along the way they stopped to settle in various locations before moving on to their final destination in the Central Valley of Mexico. A possible origin of these people was somewhere in the western part of what is today the United States, as there is a relationship between the Aztec language and that of Amerindian groups such as the Shoshoni and the Utes. However, the Aztecs could also have come from western Mexico, just west of the Central Valley. They referred to their original homeland as Azatlan, or the "Place of Reeds," and they called themselves the "Mexica," a name some scholars prefer to use when referring to them, and the origin of the names Mexico and Mexican. However, the nineteenth century historian William H. Prescott called the Mexica "Aztecs," and this has been the popular name for them ever since.

There is no civilization of pre-Columbian America about which we have as much knowledge. Unlike the Maya, the Aztecs left many written records, most of them set down just after the Spanish conquest. These histories contain myths and legends about Aztec origins that must be carefully weighed in the light of the tendency of all people to glorify their past. In addition, Spanish observers of their culture, called chroniclers, wrote about almost every feature of Aztec culture. The Spaniards found native ways shocking, scandalous, and distasteful, and had little appreciation for Amerindian cultural achievements; their writings must also be evaluated in light of their ethnocentrism and prejudice.

One of the most important documents about the Aztecs is called the *Mendoza Codex*, named for the Spanish Viceroy (governor) Don Antonio de Mendoza, who wrote down information given to him by surviving Aztecs, and drew illustrations. It is now housed in a library at Oxford University, Oxford, England, and serves as an excellent source of Aztec history, customs, and everyday life. Another important source was compiled by the Franciscan friar and chronicler Bernardino de Sahagun who, along with Indian scribes, composed a twelve volume codex, resembling an encyclopedia and covering virtually every aspect of Aztec history, religion, and daily life. Sahagun's goal was to teach other friars who were converting Amerindians to Christianity what they needed to know about Aztec ways.

In the *Mendoza Codex*, the story is told that the Aztecs reached the banks of Lake Texcoco sometime in the fourteenth century, after many years of wandering. Here they saw in the middle of the swampy marsh a huge rock, out of which was growing an

Fig. 3.2

This illustration from the Mendoza Codex, now in the Bodleian Library, Oxford University, illustrates the founding of Tenochtitlán, the city of Cactus Rock. The eagle on the cactus indicates to the founding chiefs the fulfillment of a prophecy by the god Huitzilopochtli.

enormous prickly pear cactus plant. Perched on the cactus plant was an eagle devouring a snake. (This image is preserved today on the Mexican flag and seal.) This vision was sent by the main god of the Aztecs, Huitzilopochtli ("left-handed Hummingbird"), a warrior god whose symbol was an eagle, and who may once have been a living person and a leader on the journey into the central valley. Speaking through the tribal priests, Huitzilopochtli told the Aztecs to travel until they saw just such a vision, whereupon they should settle at that site permanently.

This account of the settlement on the islands of Lake Texcoco must be weighed against other legends that do not reflect as well on the character of the Aztecs. Non-Aztec legends that survive from these years indicate that the marauding Aztecs were thoroughly detested everywhere they went. Much of this had to do with such Aztec customs as the eating of rattlesnakes and other vermin, and obsessive human sacrifice. The practice of wife- stealing was particularly distasteful to the surrounding peoples, as the Aztecs, short of women themselves, would raid neighbouring tribes for wives. Since no tribe found such people congenial as neighbours, the Aztecs were forced to settle on poor land nobody else wanted. Several stories have them hiding in the tall marsh reeds of Lake Texcoco after being routed in battle.

One of these well-known legends about the founding of what was to be the magnificent Aztec capital of Tenochtitlán had the Aztecs used as **conscripted** soldiers by one of the local warring tribes, the Colhua. Despite their despicable ways the Aztecs were

Fig. 3.3
The flag of modern-day Mexico

fierce and brutal warriors, and local tribes found them useful in battles with other tribes. The Colhua chief promised the Aztecs their freedom if they would capture eight thousand of the enemy Xochimilca people. The Aztecs defeated the Xochimilca and proceeded to kill all of their captives so as not to have to bring them back to be sacrificed to the gods of their oppressor, the Colhuac.

The ruler of the Colhuac berated the Aztecs for their cowardice in not being able to capture any victims for sacrifice to his gods. The Aztecs proceeded to dump large bags of ears cut from their victims in front of the Colhua chief, Coxcox. Surviving pictographs of this event show that the chief was disgusted, but he nevertheless kept his promise. The Aztecs then asked for a favourite daughter of chief Coxcox, in order to pay her a great honour, and invited him to attend the ceremony that would honour her and celebrate their freedom.

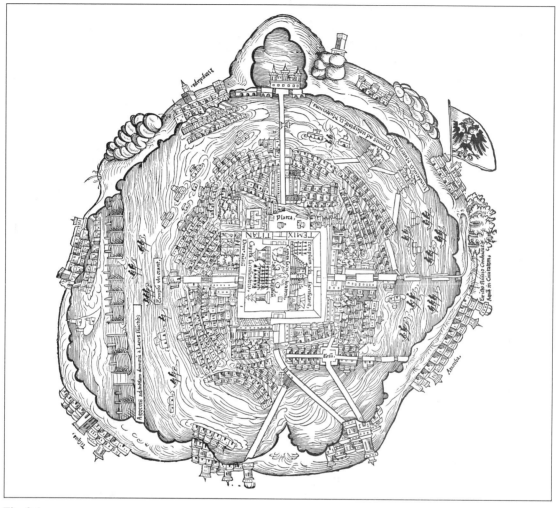

Fig. 3.4
A map of Tenochtitlán published in Nuremberg in 1524, based on a
description from a letter written by Cortés.

When the chief arrived at the temple he found an Aztec priest dancing in the flayed skin of his daughter. To the Aztecs the sacrifice of the chief's daughter and the use of her skin in a religious ceremony was a great honour, and they could not understand at all when the Coxcox called for his warriors to attack them. The Aztecs were mercilessly hunted down. Those that managed to escape took refuge on the barren, marshy islands of Lake Texcoco, where they were barely able to survive on a diet of fish, duck, and insect eggs. This miserable existence continued for a lengthy period, during which they forged the characteristics that were eventually to lead them to greatness as conquerors, the traits of unity, combativeness, and antagonism to all others.

TENOCHTITLÁN

The Aztecs called their new home Tenochtitlán, meaning "cactus growing from a rock," and in time found it a good place to live. Lake Texcoco was a salt lake two thousand metres above sea level, walled in by high mountains and fed by several lagoons of fresh water. The shallow lake itself was surrounded by thick, reedy marshes teeming with wild fowl of many varieties. Deer were found on the mountainsides, and during the rainy season, soil washed down the mountain to the lake shore, where it was used by the farmers. The Aztecs learned from their neighbours the techniques of growing corn, peppers, beans, and squash, and also learned how to trap fowl, find insect eggs, and fish for shrimp and edible algae.

Despite the contempt of their neighbours who rejoiced at their predicament, the Aztecs in time converted their swampy exile into a great city, which had about 200 000 people by the time of the Spanish conquest. Modern city planners and architects are astonished at the successful preplanning of causeways, bridges, and aqueducts. It was one of the largest cities in the world at that time, five times as large as contemporary London, England, for example. In a military alliance with two nearby city states, Tlacopan and Texcoco, the Aztecs formed *The Triple Alliance*, and came to dominate the entire central valley, setting the foundation for the eventual conquest of all Mexico. The Aztecs continued to improve Tenochtitlán by draining the marshes, eating the snakes, and steadily enlarging the livable area until the sight of it amazed the worldly wise and well-travelled Spanish soldiers, one of whom wrote:

"We were amazed . . . on account of the great towers and temples and buildings rising from the water, and all built of masonry. And some of our soldiers even asked whether the things we saw were not in a dream."

Bernal Diaz, *The Discovery and Conquest of Mexico.*

The Aztec capital city was now surrounded by good islands of farmland formed by fertile silt from the bottom of the lake and eroded soil from the mountainside, both combined with human residue. The soil was anchored by trees, and formed into fields called **chinampas**. These "floating gardens" of soil were renewed every few months with soil scraped from the bottom of Lake Texcoco and transported by canoe to the fields. Canals ran between the fields, reminding the conquering Spaniards of the canals they had seen in Venice. The islands in the lake were connected to the shore by three large causeways, raised roads across the water.

To supply the salty lake area with fresh water, the Aztecs built a dike over fifteen kilometres long from a freshwater source. Aqueducts as wide as a human body brought pure water from freshwater springs on the mainland to Tenochtitlán's reservoirs and fountains. These aqueducts were necessary because the water from the surrounding lake was too brackish and dirty for drinking or bathing. At that time in history, while the Aztecs were bathing in fresh water, bathing was unknown in many parts of Europe.

The marketplace of the Aztecs was one of the largest in the world at the time, visited by over 60 000 people each day in its clean and orderly centre. The city was also graced by several parks, gardens, aviaries, and zoos. Transportation was by dugout canoe or by foot. As there were no beasts of burden, canoes and human backs moved all loads. Tenochtitlán was a constant hubbub of activity, with marches, sacrifices, and steady streams of load-bearers and runners.

The most important part of Tenochtitlán was the huge pyramid in its centre, surrounded by temples and buildings, all enclosed by a high wall covered with serpent decorations. It was to this central pyramid that all roads, canals, and causeways led. The pyramid was topped by two temples and a large level area. In one of the two temples at the summit stood the statue of the quetzal-feathered War God, with hearts of silver draped around its neck. The area was overseen by priests covered in dark, hooded robes matted with human blood from sacrifices. For religious reasons the priests could never wash or change their clothing, and so the entire pyramid summit gave off a rotten stench of human blood and death. Other pyramid-topped temples, called *teocalli*, were located around the city and served similar purposes.

The striking architecture of the *teocalli* gave the illusion of great height and mass. Stepped terraces placed at various locations around the structures had the effect of making the viewer at ground level feel as if the stairs were leading to the heavens. The level

summits could not be seen from the base of the building, and this fact contributed to the sense of height, mystery, and nearness to the gods. Congregations of worshippers stood in the plaza below the pyramid-temple, unprotected from the sun or the weather, to worship at the shrine. When great processions climbed the stairs, it must have seemed to the Aztecs below as if the line of marchers were disappearing into the heavens.

Modern Mexico City has been built on the site of the Aztec capital of Tenochtitlán. Between the years 1978 to 1982 a Mexican archaeological team under E. M. Moctezuma excavated the area of the temple pyramid, the pyramid itself having been dismantled by the Spanish conquerors to provide building material for a Spanish cathedral. The excavations unearthed numerous Aztec artifacts as well as the bones of sacrificed children, whose tears were thought by the Aztecs to move the god and bring rain. Several different reconstructions of the temple over a period of two centuries were also revealed. Most of what is known about Tenochtitlán is derived from immediate post-conquest accounts, as any extensive archaeological excavations at the site of the former Aztec city would cause massive disruption of life in modern Mexico City.

HOUSES IN TENOCHTITLÁN

The Aztecs were fond of bright colours. Walls, murals, and carvings were painted blue, green, black, and red. This brightness was only on the exterior of the buildings, however, as the insides were dark and gloomy in order to repel invasion by monstrous gods. Rooms had no windows, only slits high up to let smoke escape.

The narrow streets of the city were lined with simple mud and reed houses. These houses were squat, with flat roofs, made attractive by flowers planted in between homes and on roofs. Floors were stamped earth covered by deer skin, and there was no door, only a cloth hanging over the opening to keep out the elements. Homes were built around patios and were often expanded in a haphazard and rambling way as the need arose. Some of the better homes, such as that of the fabled King Moctezuma II, were made of red stone; they also used woods that gave off a pleasant aroma, such as cedar, for the ceiling. The walls were decorated with beautiful featherwork, cotton fabrics, and animal skins. These better homes would have colourful flower gardens, aviaries, and plants of medicinal value. Houses were separated by canals, and wooden planks were laid across the canals to enable people to cross.

In this crowded city, as in all cities, sanitation was a problem. The Aztecs dealt with this by tying up canoes at strategic locations along the shore, to be used as public washrooms. When the canoe was filled, the contents were then sold to the nearby farmers for use as fertilizer. Urine was deposited in pottery vessels to be used as gold dye for cloth. A sewer system based on gravity flushed excess human wastes into the rapidly polluting lake. This feat of sanitary engineering was unmatched anywhere else in the world at the time.

PHYSICAL APPEARANCE

Like most Amerindians, Aztec males averaged between 65 cm and 75 cm in height; women were several centimetres shorter. They all had dark and abundant hair, but not on the face or body. The Aztecs were practically beardless. The Aztec's skin colour ranged from dark to light brown, the nose was prominent, and the eyes were almond-shaped. Commoners dressed day and night in a simple loincloth passed between the legs and tied together around the waist. All women wore the same pattern of dress: an ankle-length underskirt covered by a poncho-like dress of beautiful colours in an endless variety of woven patterns. Most Aztecs wore no shoes, but wealthier citizens wore sandals, and the emperor wore sandals of gold.

THE FIERCE RELIGION OF THE AZTECS

As in other Amerindian cultures, religion played a dominant role in the everyday life of the Aztecs. The traditions of their religion went back to Olmec times, traditions subsequently adopted and reinterpreted by every Mesoamerican civilization. Every moment of life from birth to death was overseen by the gods and was intertwined with religious rituals under the control of a learned priesthood. Several main gods were in ascendency in the Aztec world, each representing four different creations before the creation of the present world. Each creation was ruled over by its own god, and and each

Fig. 3.5
An artist's impression of what Tenochtitlán would have looked like.

world had succumbed to a different disaster — fire, wind, or waters. The Aztecs predicted the eventual destruction of their own civilization, the fifth creation.

The current world of the Aztecs, the Fifth Sun, came to pass when the the twin arch rival gods, Quetzalcoatl, or "Plumed-serpent," and Tezcatlipoca, or "Smoking-mirror" (named for the mysterious black, glass-like mirror that did not allow magicians to look into it in order to foretell the future), descended to the earth with the terrible goddess of the earth Tlaltecuhtli. The twin creator gods changed into giant serpents and grabbed the earth goddess, who was in the form of a giant alligator with enormous jaguar claws and fangs, and snapping mouths at the arm and leg joints, and broke her in two pieces. One piece became the earth, the other went back to the heavens to bring forth some 800 gods and the planets.

Other gods were summoned by the moans and cries from the destroyed carcase of the earth goddess, and they came down to earth to comfort her. They soothed her by commanding that from her body would come all fruits for the earth's future human populace. Mountains and valleys would come from her mouth, ponds from her eyes, rivers from her nose, and trees and other flowers and plants from her skin and hair. Now the new and fifth world was ready for humans, and would be created by Quetzalcoatl from the rotting bodies of the dead of previous creations. However, the dying earth goddess continued to cry and commanded that she be repaid for her sacrifice by the blood and the hearts of living victims.

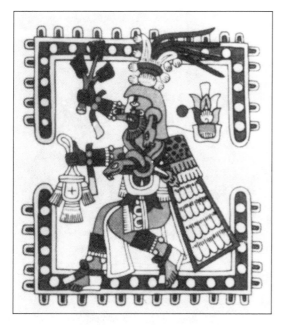

Fig. 3.6
Quetzlcoatl as conceived by an Aztec artist.

The earth was now complete, and so each of the gods vied for the privilege of being the ruling Sun God. As each one threw itself upon a fire, the purity of the fire would reject it for its pride. Finally, an unhappy and poor young man whose body was covered with warts filled with yellow pus was chosen. He too needed human blood, the most valuable offering any human could make, to strengthen him for the difficult journey each day across the sky and each night into the womb of his earth goddess mother. Only a very few would need to be sacrificed daily to keep the sun moving in the sky, but such sacrifice must never be completely halted or it would result in the sun dying of thirst from the great heat.

THE ROLE OF HUMAN SACRIFICE IN THE AZTEC RELIGION

Human sacrifice came to play an important role in the religion of the Aztecs. The sun provided the light and warmth necessary to the growing of corn and other foods. The Aztecs believed that without human blood and human hearts, the sun and other celestial bodies would no longer move in the sky, and the human race would perish in the fire that would result. To die in sacrifice to the sun was to be privileged to die an honourable and even glorious death. After all, did not the sun itself sacrifice its own victims each morning — as it rose in the sky, the stars died.

The practice of human sacrifice seems extraordinarily cruel and unnecessarily brutal. However, every culture at every period of history has defined cruelty in a different way. The Aztecs were not the only people in Mesoamerica to practise human sacrifice. In fact, ritual sacrifice of human beings was common throughout the ancient New World, if not to the same extent as with the Aztecs. During their early wanderings the Aztecs had stayed for a time at the ruined Toltec city of Tula, and they had come to revere the Toltecs as a great artistic people of a golden age. Although their notions about the Toltecs were based largely on myth, half-truth, and legend, part of their reverence took the form of emulating the Toltec practice of human sacrifice.

At least it can be said that the human sacrifice of the Aztecs was not motivated by intolerance or hatred, but by a deeply held religious belief of the necessity of the blood in order to save life on earth. The Aztecs did not hate their victims; in fact they respected them, even envied them the privilege of being sacrificed. From the time of capture until the day of death, the victim was treated as royalty, was fed well, and worshipped. When the time for sacrifice came, the victim would be led up the stairs of the pyramid-temple, the priests holding tightly to his arms, legs, and head. A priest in a scarlet robe would plunge a sharp obsidian blade deep into his chest, give it a powerful twist, and with his hands tear out the heart. The priest would lift the heart up to the sun, and then toss it at the feet or in the open jaws of the stone god of the temple.

Other common sacrificial methods included decapitation, burning alive, drowning, strangling, skinning alive, being thrown from a great height, starving, being impaled on a rock, being shot by arrows, and having one's head crushed by a rock. It is important to realize that most Aztec sacrifice involved at least the partial willingness and co-operation of the victim, who shared the belief in the need for the celestial bodies to have human blood in order to keep moving in the sky.

The priests led withdrawn lives and had no contact with women. They were held in deep reverence by the public. They ate mushrooms that induced hallucinations, and these may have been responsible for their strange vision of life. They never cut their blood-soaked hair or fingernails, and never bathed. During a one-day orgy of celebrating the dedication of the temple, in the reign of the emperor Ahuizotl, it is estimated that 10 000-20 000 were sacrificed by

Fig. 3.7
In this picture from the Florentine Codex, an Aztec priest raises a freshly removed human heart to the sun god. In the Aztec religion the sun required a fresh supply of sacrificial human blood every day.

what was virtually an assembly line of priests, and the waters of Lake Texcoco ran red with the blood of victims. The entire city of Tenochtitlán was rank with the odour of death, and disease broke out among the population.

In the early sixteenth century the Spanish conquistadore Hernan Cortés and his men were the only non-Amerindians ever to witness the human sacrifice of the Aztecs, as this practice ended once the empire was conquered. The human sacrifice of the Aztecs has fascinated both scholar and layman ever since. Some historians estimate the rate of victims at over 20 000 per year. The standard explanation for this terrible phenomenon has been that the gods of the Aztecs demanded such sacrifice in order to sustain life, and so the Aztecs had no choice if they hoped to survive. One writer on the subject, however, Michael Harner, has suggested the interesting but highly controversial possibility of the impact of the ecological circumstances of the Aztecs.

A CONTROVERSIAL EXPLANATION OF THE PLACE OF HUMAN SACRIFICE IN AZTEC CULTURE

Harner proposes that in prehistoric times, as the population in both the Old World and the New began to grow, overhunting caused many big game animals to die out. People were forced to shift to fishing and to hunting small game. Eventually, even the supply of small game could not provide the increasing human populations with sufficient food, and this lack of sufficient game was one of the causes of the domestication of plants and animals. The Old World had **herbivorous** mammals such as pigs, cattle, and sheep that could be domesticated and fed on natural pasture. But in most of the New World, herbivorous animals had long since died out, and there were no animals suitable for domestication. This was particularly true in Mesoamerica and Mexico, where even the guinea pig, the llama, and

the alpaca (found in the Andean region of Peru) had long been extinct. Some dogs, and wildfowl such as turkey, were bred for protein, but these were far from satisfactory solutions to the problem.

In the Valley of Mexico the Aztecs faced a serious protein problem as their population continued to grow and as the supply of protein diminished. It is Harner's hypothesis that cannibalism, disguised as sacrifice, was the only natural solution to the problem. It is estimated that the Aztecs may have sacrificed up to 250 000 victims in peak years of the fifteenth century, raising the question of what was done with the bodies of the victims. The Spanish conquistadores wrote about the Aztec practice of waging wars strictly for the purpose of obtaining victims for sacrifice. Some of the conquered warriors would be eaten on the battlefield, when after a particularly successful battle soldiers would stuff themselves to the point of being unable to walk. Others were put in wooden cages and fattened up before their sacrifice, their remains to be served as a delicacy on special occasions.

The ceremony of sacrifice was carried out by priests in the pyramid- temple. This rite, as we have seen, involved cutting out the heart of the victim and offering the blood-drenched organ to the gods. The head was placed on a skull rack and the corpse was sent tumbling down the stairs of the pyramid, stairs already covered with congealed blood. Three of the limbs of the victim belonged to the warrior who had captured him, and these limbs were later consumed in tomato and pepper stew at the warrior's living quarters. The rest of the torso was taken to the zoo and fed to carnivorous mammals, snakes, and birds. All ancient Amerindians who engaged in cannibalism believed that such qualities as courage and wisdom reside in human flesh and can be obtained by others through its consumption. Such cannibalism, however, coincidentally provided the Aztecs with proteins, fats, and amino acids, elements of diet that they were lacking.

Such an explanation, of course, is highly controversial, and by its nature cannot be proven. In Harner's view, however, it explains aspects of Aztec culture that are difficult to understand otherwise, such as the high motivation of the fighting force (to obtain protein), the steepness of the pyramid stairs (to allow the bodies to roll down more easily), and the seeming obsession of the Aztecs with human sacrifice. To Harner, the Aztecs were a people responding to a dietary need for survival.

Harner's hypothesis has provoked much controversy. Since its publication in 1977, there have been many attacks on it, and some alternative theses have been proposed (*see Bibliography at end of chapter*).

WARFARE

War was the primary purpose of the Aztec state. The Aztecs seized upon their mission of warfare with a belligerent enthusiasm rarely matched in human history. They were always able to find an excuse or pretext to wage war, be it an imagined insult, an interference with the travel of their merchants, or a refusal to pay extortionate tribute.

All able-bodied men of fighting age were part of the Aztec force, including priests and merchants. The latter were involved in drawing maps based on their travels and gathering information about enemies. The greatest glory for the Aztec fighter was to provide captives for the state, or to die in battle. An elite corps of veterans fought in the front of the army. The entire army moved forward in rows at the sound of shell trumpets blown by priests. The primary objective of each soldier in battle was to isolate an enemy soldier and move him to the Aztec rear, where he would be eventually taken to Tenochtitlán for sacrifice.

The officer's uniform was a jaguar skin arrayed with the feathers of the warrior's fighting order, for example the Eagle or Jaguar knights. The common soldier, or *macehuales*, was less well clothed, but all soldiers wore a quilted cotton armour. The Aztec warriors used flat spears with very sharp blades of obsidian (a glass-like volcanic rock found in great abundance in Mesoamerica), deadly clubs with sharp obsidian blades along the sides, and darts flung from a kind of spear thrower called an *atlatl*. The *macahuitl*, the spears and clubs, could decapitate a soldier with one blow. The soldiers carried shields decorated with colourful feathers. Arrows, stones, and darts would be hurled at them, but they would be easily deflected by the shields. Armies would march forward while whistling and shouting war cries. When the last of the enemy had been captured or cut to pieces, the temple of the enemy tribe would be burned to the ground.

As most of the conquered groups spoke the same language as the Aztecs — *Nahuatl* — and worshipped similar gods, the Aztecs tended to absorb the gods of the

Fig. 3.8
This page from the
Mendoza Codex shows
various rankings of Aztec
warriors taking captives.

conquered into their own pantheon. Most of the conquered tribe would be spared but would be required to pay heavy tribute in the form of corn, metals, slaves, and jade (considered more valuable than gold); the conquered province of Cuauhititlan, for example, was required to provide annually 62 feathered shields, 62 warrior costumes, 4000 reed mats and seats, 1200 cotton cloaks, and large amounts of corn, beans, and other produce. In the light of this it is not hard to understand why many of the conquered tribes so readily aided the Spanish when Cortés marched to Tenochtitlán.

Around the middle of the fifteenth century a string of natural disasters struck the Valley of Mexico. Several years of drought were followed by years of killing frosts and heavy snows. People starved when the corn crop, the staple of the diet, failed. This cycle of climate change was common in the area, but was not within the memory of any of the tribes, who took it to mean that the gods were unhappy. The emperor of the most powerful tribe, Moctezuma I of the Aztecs, determined to appease the gods with more sacrificial victims than ever before. He embarked on a reign of terror that did not end until more than 10 000 had been slaughtered.

The tragedy was that this orgy of sacrifice coincided with the return of warm weather and a flourishing corn crop. In the eyes of the Amerindians, appeasing the gods seemed to have worked. After this, the purpose of warfare changed from a desire for conquest and tribute to a quest for victims for sacrifice. Capturing a soldier for sacrifice to supply the hungry gods became more glorious than killing enemies in battle.

As virtually all the tribes of this era were dominated by a similar war-like spirit and worshipped blood-hungry gods, perpetual **"flower wars"** were the logical result of this change. Enemies would meet in a pre-arranged battlefield to fight strictly for the purpose of taking captives for sacrifice. 'Flowers' was a metaphor for human blood and the field of battle was a field of flowers. After a certain time the fighting would be ended by the agreement of both sides that each had all the captives necessary. The flower wars, found nowhere else as a type of battle, was unique in all of recorded human history.

Such battles could not have taken place without the widespread consensus of the people, and even the victims, that such tactics were necessary. Many war-like societies believe that the way a man dies is more important than the way he lives, and to the warriors, dying as a sacrifice was a most honourable death. Some victims took part in a "gladiatorial combat" just before their sacrifice, where they would be handicapped in some way, such as being sent unarmed into combat with several armed captors in a narrow field. If the captive fought well he might win his freedom, although some still preferred to die for the glory of the gods.

It was the Aztecs who were the most inspired and best organized of the warrior tribes of the valley of central Mexico. As the decades wore on, Aztec warriors enjoyed victory after victory, and by 1440 they were the most wealthy and powerful tribe in the Valley of Mexico. It would not be the last time in history that a small, talented, and determined island people came to dominate a region much larger than their population or resources seemed to allow.

THE AZTECS IN POWER

Following the settlement on the islands of Lake Texcoco, and up to the Spanish conquest, the Aztecs consolidated their power in the central part of Mexico. A few tribes were not conquered by the Aztecs, notably the neighbouring Tlaxcalans and Tarascans, who were able to refuse the demands for victims for sacrifice and for heavy tribute; they remained independent up to the time of the Spanish conquest. The reason the Tarascans had never been conquered by the Aztecs was their discovery of the use of bronze for weapons. Some historians believe that had the Spanish conquest not taken place, the Aztec empire might have been conquered within 50 years by the Tarascans as they improved this weaponry. In the end, they allied themselves with the invaders and helped bring about the downfall of the Aztecs.

Once a tribe had been conquered, the Aztecs proceeded to rewrite history in order to glorify the humble beginnings of their people. An adviser to Aztec emperors named Tlacelel, at the beginning of the Aztec period of conquest, had the books of all conquered tribes destroyed by burning. New histories were written describing the Aztecs as a people of destiny, heirs of the great Mayan and Toltec traditions. This re-writing of history helped the Aztecs become more confident than ever in their mission,

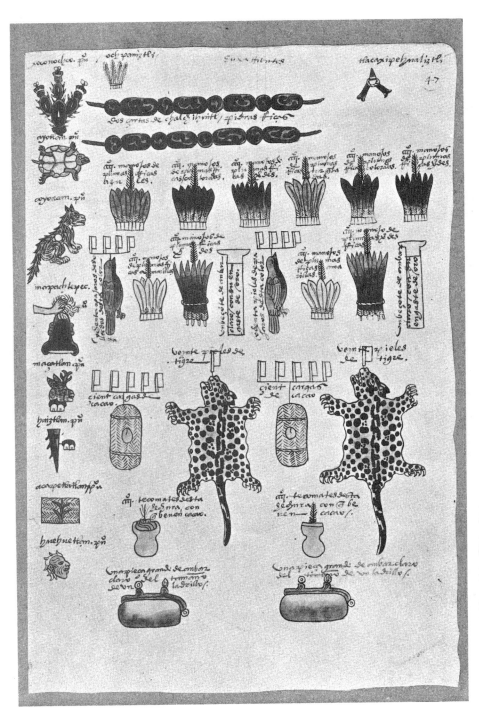

Fig. 3.9
This birch-bark page from a Codex represents a record of items received in tribute from a conquered town. Items shown include bowls, jars of honey, precious stones, warsuits, headdresses, and beads.

making them an even more difficult rival for their enemies. (Such rewriting of history is not unknown, of course, in our century, especially in totalitarian societies even to this day. Even democratic societies have difficulty at times with writing objective histories of their own wars, scandals, etc.)

After inflicting a military defeat and taking a large number of sacrificial victims from the conquered people, the Aztecs would usually place the defeated leader or one of his dynasty back on the throne, and require the subject people to pay tribute. This loose domination was convenient because it allowed the Aztecs to wage occasional war on the conquered people in order to obtain more captives for sacrifice. The conquered tribes were forced to view the Aztec sacrifices; this had a salutary effect and helped to keep the subject tribes docile.

THE CASTE SYSTEM

By 1500 the Aztecs had developed a **caste system**. At the bottom were the slaves, called **tlacotli**, who came from prisoners of war deemed not fit for sacrifice, and from the criminal classes of the society. These slaves may be compared with their contemporaries in Europe, the serfs, in that they farmed the land of the Aztec nobility. In general they were well treated and were freed upon the death of their owner. A slave's children were born free, and he could own slaves himself while still a slave. The majority of the people were of the caste of commoners called **macehualli**; they farmed lands held in common in groups or clans. At the top of the system were the noblemen, or **pipiltin**, from whom came the admin-

istrators of the empire. All Aztecs considered themselves kin, and there was little tension among the classes. The nobility saw themselves, and were seen by commoners, as kindly people who would use their wealth and power for good.

Outside of this rigid caste system, rigid in the sense that a person was born and died in the same caste — there was no social mobility — stood two important groups. One was the warriors, who were rewarded with their own lands, and the other was the *pochteca*, a hereditary guild of armed merchants who carried on trade, travelling long distances into foreign territories with heavy loads on their backs, and bringing back to the royal palace luxuries like jaguar skins, jade, and quetzal plumes not available in the homeland. The *pochteca* were equally important in gathering intelligence data to be used in future wars. Occasionally, when the Aztecs wanted to start a war, the *pochteca* would act as *agents-provocateur*, provoking trouble.

THE EMPEROR AND HIGH OFFICIALS

At the pinnacle of the caste system stood the emperor and high government officials. They ruled without concern for democracy in any modern sense, as freedom of thought and speech and the rights of the individual were concepts unknown to the Aztec mind. Although he was elected and advised by a council, the emperor had a semi-divine status. He had unrestricted power in the realm of foreign policy, especially in diplomacy, as commander of the army, and in collecting tribute and warfare. He was worshipped

Fig. 3.10

Plundered from Moctezuma's empire by the Spaniards and sent back to Spain, this 1.3 m high headdress made of rare quetzal bird tail feathers shows the beautiful craftsmanship of Aztec featherwork. The feathers are woven into the cloth, and blue feathers and tiny pieces of gold fringe the bottom.

as a **demigod**, and all who came into his presence had to dress in rags, remain unshod, and humble themselves by bowing and scraping before him without looking at his face. He was carried on a litter covered with precious feathers everywhere he went, and the way in front of him would be swept by nobles and covered with cloths, so that if he walked his feet would not touch the dirt.

At meals he could choose from several hundred dishes while being entertained by jugglers, clowns, and dwarves. Servants would rush forward with a clean napkin as soon as one was dirtied by the emperor, in order that a soiled one never touched his lips. At some particularly important banquets a slaughtered slave or sacrificed captive might be served. The last emperor before the Spanish arrival, Moctezuma II, had beautiful hanging gardens and palaces, and a royal zoo of rare animals and exotic birds from all over the empire. He changed his elaborate and intricate costumes four times a day. The life of the emperor has been referred to by one author as a life of "barbaric pageantry."

Other officials of the government included judges, generals, governors, and neighbourhood chiefs. These men were usually appointed by the emperor on the basis of their qualifications, and as a result of their appointments could live in palaces with many slaves, dress in feathered finery, and be spared from paying taxes.

ECONOMY

All this extravagance was made possible by the strong Aztec agricultural base, which produced large crops of beans, squash, corn, tomatoes, and other vegetables. The Aztecs used primitive digging sticks, stone chisels, and stone axes to farm, although some of these were eventually replaced by tools of copper and obsidian. Corn was the staple crop, but cacao beans, used in making chocolate and also as a medium of exchange, were very important. The emperor and his retinue consumed enormous quantities of a chocolate drink made from the cacao bean. Chocolate at this time was unknown in Europe and was one of many crops, including corn, beans, pumpkins, squash, tomatoes, peppers, and tobacco introduced into Europe after the conquest.

One important crop was a cactus known as maguey; its pulp and fibre were fermented into a nutritious alcoholic drink called **pulque**. Officially *pulque* was available only for ritual purposes and for the old, with a sort of unofficial allowance made for older alcoholics. There were very harsh laws against drunkenness, yet the student of history must ask why this was necessary if *pulque* was not readily available. The suspicion is that drunkenness was a problem, perhaps similar in the way alcoholism was a problem in the days of American and Canadian Prohibition. The roots of the maguey plant were used in making thread and the

cord used in sandals, and the thorns of the plant were used for pins and needles. Even the leaves were used as thatch for roofs.

Because good land was hard to come by, some Aztecs scraped soil from the lakebed and placed it on floating rafts made of reeds tightly tied together. Some of these rafts held a hut and a caretaker who steered with a long pole. On these rafts farmers grew the food that helped to create a surplus of wealth in the empire.

Every day thousands of canoes would travel the lake bringing goods to Tenochtitlán for tribute or for trade. Every fifth day a large market would be held in the plaza of Tenochtitlán, offering textiles, pottery, feather head-dresses, real and paper flowers, and other craft works. Grocery stalls were well stocked with a huge choice of game and produce. Slaves were bought and sold. Some forty thousand shoppers thronged to the plaza each day; the Spaniards were amazed at the wide variety of goods. Each village had its own market on a smaller scale, which was the centre of social life just as it is today in many regions of Amerindian Mexico.

Another important aspect of the Aztec economy was long-distance trade. Among the Aztec nobles there was a great demand for luxury goods such as rare skins and feathers. These were all obtained from areas remote from the Mexican heartland, mostly from the coastal lowlands of the Gulf of Mexico and the Mayan area. This tremendous demand for luxury goods almost certainly fuelled the desire to expand the empire to the south.

CRIME AND PUNISHMENT

It is natural that in a society where warfare played such an important role, violence and bloodshed were part of the way of life. Laws for all citizens were strictly enforced, and the most common form of punishment was death by stoning, hanging, burning alive, or drowning. The Aztecs did not have prisons, only wooden cages for those awaiting death. There were few written legal codes. Most crimes consisted of breaking tradition or discipline, and this included everything from cowardly behaviour to bad manners. Religious crimes, such as the robbing of temples, were considered the most heinous, because they could provoke the gods into vengeful actions. Murder was not considered as serious a crime as breaking the unwritten tribal codes of discipline. Punishment for breaking tradition was not imposed by rulers but demanded by public consensus.

THE AZTEC CALENDAR

One of the greatest pre-Columbian archaeological finds was the discovery in 1790 in Mexico City of the great Aztec calendar stone, a twenty-tonne black stone in the shape of a disk. It stood in front of the Temple of the Sun. Its calendar was closely followed by all Aztecs. The stone was also likely used as a platform for human sacrifice. On it is carved a great deal of information in pictures about the Aztec interpretation of the history of the world, and it has provided historians with a wealth of information about Aztec culture. It was buried in or about 1560 by the Spanish archbishop of Mexico, who feared that the Amerindians he was attempting to convert to Christianity would be inspired to continue to practise their old religion by its awesome presence. It was discovered during the construction of a great cathedral, and the Spanish had it built into the wall of a church, where it remained until 1885, when it was finally removed to a museum.

The Aztec calendar was not as advanced as the Mayan calendar, although priests carried out detailed observations of the sun, moon , planets, and stars, and their knowledge of astronomy was considerably greater than their knowledge of any other science. The calendar dominated the daily life of the Aztec people. Actually the Aztecs had two calendars working simultaneously, the *Almanac year* and the *Solar year*. The *Almanac year* was used for ritual purposes and each day in its 260-day year was surrounded with superstitions of either good or bad tidings. If a child were born on a bad day the priests would wait until a good day to name him or her. Weeks were thirteen days long, and each had special ceremonies. The religious rituals of the Almanac year provided meaning and excitement in the daily life of the ordinary Aztecs. Citizens would be involved in decorating statues of gods, singing and dancing, feasting, and playing musical instruments. As always, much human sacrifice would take place.

The *Solar year* was based on the earth-sun relationship and was designed as an accurate measurement of time. The *solar year* comprised 18 months of 20 days each, with 5 extra days. These final five days were particularly unlucky and many Aztecs re-

Fig. 3.11
The great Aztec calendar stone was buried by the Spanish conquerors in the fifteenth century and was not rediscovered until the late eighteenth century. For nearly a century afterwards, this important artifact was simply propped up against a cathedral wall in Mexico City, the Spanish City that arose on the ruins of Tenochtitlán. Originally the calendar stone was painted with many bright colours.

mained in their homes until they were over. When these days came at the end of a 52-year cycle, comparable to a century in our way of thinking, people lived in mortal fear of the coming of a great natural catastrophe. After a period of 104 solar years, the two calendars would coincide. This was the most dangerous time of all as the sun might be destroyed. All fires in all temples, homes, and palaces would have to be extinguished during this time in order for the universe to continue.

One festival was the the annual sacrifice to the god Tezcatlipoca. A handsome young warrior would be selected one year in advance to play the role of this god. For a year he would be dressed up and painted like the god, and would play tunes from a bone flute hanging about his neck. Four beautiful wives would follow him everywhere. Finally, on the appointed day he willingly mounted the pyramid steps to be placed on his back for the sacrificial removal of his heart. It was considered an honour to be chosen to play this role.

WRITING

Aztec writing was not as advanced or sophisticated as the writing of the Maya. Everything the Aztecs wrote about had to be shown in picture form, and thus the Aztec form of writing is known as **pictograph writing**. The Maya could show ideas abstractly by their glyphs, and so their writing is known as **ideograph writing**. Ideographs had been forgotten by the time of the Aztecs, even by the Maya who lived during the time of the Aztec empire.

Some Aztec writing survives to this day on animal skin or cloth. Most Aztec books were scrolls of fibre made from the maguey plant, the plant used in making the alcoholic beverage *pulque*. These books would be folded into a bundle much like a fan is folded.

As every action had to be shown by a picture in Aztec writing, the manuscripts were covered with little human forms scurrying about all over the place. The human shape itself, because it was used so often, was drawn hastily, with a large head and a small body; the body part doing the action was the most conspicuous part.

Like Mayan numbering, Aztec numbering was based on the vigesimal system of twenty, and numbers were shown by dots for the numbers 1 to 19, a flag for 20, a facsimile of a pine tree for 400, and an incense pouch for 8000.

Some men with a talent for drawing would be trained from a young age as **scribes**, and they would write and record history, chronology, laws, accounts of tribute, and maps, as well as fables and myths.

There may have been hundreds of books in the Aztec library by the time of the arrival of the Spanish, but the foreign invaders destroyed most of them. They considered them ungodly and dangerous to the missionary work of the Spanish priests.

About forty Aztec books have survived to our time, and unlike the obscure Mayan glyphs, they have been for the most part successfully deciphered. Some of the writing, however, depended upon what anthropologists call an **oral tradition** that required the reader to fill in missing backgrounds, details, nuances, and other things; these writings would be understandable only to a reader steeped in the culture.

AN AZTEC CHILDHOOD

The purpose of a child's life was clearly proclaimed at birth. A newborn baby boy was pledged immediately, by the midwife who delivered him, to the battlefield. He was dedicated to the service of the Sun God, and his first gift was a tiny bow and arrows. A girl was pledged to work hard beside the family hearth, to grind corn, and to prepare drinks. At her birth her first gifts were tiny spinning and weaving implements. **Sex roles** were clearly reinforced from an early age. If a mother died in childbirth, a not unusual occurrence, she would be deified like a warrior slain in battle. Some warriors would try to cut off the middle finger from her corpse as an amulet, a good luck charm that would ensure safety and luck on the field of battle.

During early childhood, children lived with loving parents who taught them practical tasks such as spinning cloth for girls and hauling water or firewood for boys. Punishment was firm and was often in the form of forcing the child to inhale the smoke of hot, burning chili peppers. Occasionally a child was punished by being scratched or punctured by a cactus thorn. Boy and girl children were separated at a very young age, and girls were punished for even talking to a boy. Youngsters had to memorize and then recite long lists of their duties, and in these ways were **socialized** at an early age into the customs of their society.

All Aztec children were trained through their education to dedicate themselves unquestioningly to the Aztec life of war and religion. Sons and daughters of the nobles left home early and were placed in a strict school called a **calmecac**, where they dedicated their lives to the beloved god Quetzalcoatl, and were taught to act with reserve and humility. At this school students worked hard in the fields, fasted frequently, and were punished often for breaking any of the severe rules. For the boys, sleep was often interrupted for middle of the night hikes into the mountains for ritual shedding of blood from self-inflicted wounds. The children slept on bare floors, and were forced to survive cold and hunger. At this school, also, priests taught the elaborate rituals surrounding time and the calendar.

The sons of the common people were sent to schools that were less severe; here they learned to dedicate themselves to the "Warrior God." For a boy who failed to become a warrior, the prospect was slavery or death, as there was no other occupation

for a young commoner. By the age of fifteen young men were sent into battle as messengers or transporters, and became hardened to war. Young men stayed in school until they captured an enemy in combat or took a wife, both signs of reaching adulthood in the tribe. For girls, only a small amount of education was necessary, as they played no role at all in government or the military. Only religious duties and the arts of cooking and weaving were important for them to learn, and these were mostly taught to them by their mothers. They were expected never to interfere in the business of the men, and they were required to live lives of unquestioned chastity and virtue.

When the young men had completed their education they graduated by listening to long speeches from the priests about what to do and what not to do to be a good Aztec. At this point they were expected to marry, and a bride would be carried on the back of an older woman to the home of the groom, where bride and groom would both sit on mats. Elders at each of the four corners of the mat would give them advice on how to live. *Pulque* and chocolate were drunk in large quantities by those older than middle age, but younger people had to omit the *pulque* as they were not allowed to be intoxicated. At this point childhood was over and men assumed the responsibilities of adult members of the tribe, paying taxes, working on the land or in the city, supporting a family, and going to war when needed.

Polygamy was often practised in warrior societies in which brides were often widowed at a young age, and where there was a shortage of men. Most Aztec men could

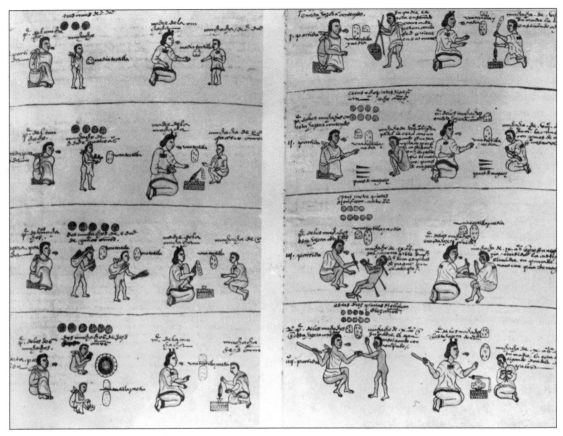

Fig. 3.12
These pages from the Mendoza Codex show various stages in the education of an Aztec child. The age of the child is shown by the number of dots. The picture on the left of each column shows a boy's education; the picture on the right illustrates a girl's education. Various punishments are also shown.

only afford one wife, but wealthier nobles might have several wives. The first bride was the mistress of the home, but other wives were well treated and were often the close friends of the first wife. There was a double standard of sexual behaviour, as girls and wives had to be chaste and faithful, but a man was allowed relations outside of marriage.

DEATH AND BURIAL

Death and burial in Aztec society reflected the belief that death merely meant passage from an earthly existence to a mysterious new existence in a new universe. One destination of the dead was the Land of the Dead, the place for those who died a natural death. A beautiful green, warm land with everlasting spring — the Land of the Rain Gods — was the destination for anyone killed by a disaster, such as lightning, drowning, or certain diseases. A third destination was "Heaven," reserved for those who died in war or were sacrificed, and for mothers who died in childbirth.

As in many religions today, mourning was designed to ease the burden of sorrow on the mourners, and to prepare the body for its journey. A comforting eulogy was delivered. The body was then carefully wrapped in a soft bark paper before being burned. Personal belongings were burned with the corpse in order to envelope it in smoke for protection against the wind on its journey. Often a small dog was burned along with the body as a guide for the four-year journey of the dead. A green stone was placed in the mouth of the corpse, jade for nobles, a lesser stone for commoners, to become a new heart in the new life. The charred bones were placed in a jar and buried beneath the home of the dead person. If the dead person had many slaves, some might be sacrificed to serve their master in death as well as in life. Four years after death, some of the dead would be chosen as companions of the sun and would return to earth as beautiful hummingbirds and butterflies, spending eternity living off sweet plant nectar.

GAMES

Games were part of religious ritual and included the sacred ball game played all over the southern part of North America, a variation of the game described in the chapter on the Maya. This game, called *tlachtli* by the Aztecs, was played from Arizona to Honduras, and had a ritual significance that was underlined by its being played within full sight of racks of skulls from sacrificial victims.

Another popular game was the *volador*, where men dressed like birds were attached by ropes to high poles and were spun in a wide circle thirteen times around the pole, as if they were flying. A game that had less religious significance and was used more for gambling was called *patolli*; it resembled our board games such as backgammon and parcheesi. In fact, Cortés played this game with Moctezuma II when the latter was held captive by the Spaniards.

OTHER ASPECTS OF AZTEC CULTURE: JEWELRY, POETRY, MUSIC, MEDICINE

The most valuable of all stones to the Aztecs was jade, called *chalchihuite*. This green stone had far more value than gold or silver, both of which the Aztecs only used for crafts. It was the green jade that had true beauty in their eyes, and nobles wore it to indicate their high rank. Jade nose, lip, and ear plugs were worn as jewelry; some jade plugs stretched the earlobe down to the shoulder of the wearer. Commoners could not even own jade, it was so prestigious. Gold was valued mainly for its ability to be moulded into many shapes. The gold jewelry that has survived shows a high artistic

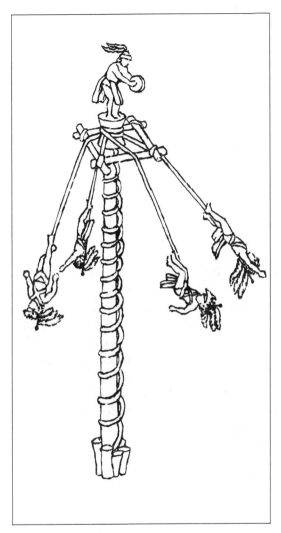

Fig. 3.13
The *volador*, a type of flywheel game, was, like so many ancient games, part sport, part ceremony. The players spun rapidly around the wheel, giving the impression of flying. Variations of this game are still performed in Mexico today.

level. The methods of crafting precious stones were, as in many societies, passed from father to son. Unfortunately, even until the middle of this century, many western-

ners did not see any artistic merit in Meso-american art, and many gold masterpieces of Aztec art were routinely melted down into gold for bullion.

The Aztecs were a poetic people, and young noblemen memorized and wrote poetry and songs. A few fragmentary pre-conquest examples of poetry have survived, and these, along with post-conquest Aztec poetry, show sensitivity and grace. Musical instruments played by the Aztecs included reeds, flutes, drums, and rattles. To the modern ear the Aztec music that has come down to us is monotonous, although it may be that more varied music existed that did not survive the conquest.

Medicine was not practised exclusively by priests, as it was in other deeply religious and magical societies. Natural healing was the goal of treatment, and careful observations were made of all medicinal treatments with herbs in order to see which ones might better help the next time. Cleanliness was stressed as being of medicinal value. It has been suggested that Aztec medicine was superior to European medicine at this time.

Measured against their own time, Aztec achievements were considerable, particularly in light of their humble beginnings. Their skill in warfare cannot be discounted. But their religion, and the deference each Aztec paid to the tribe at the cost of any individual initiative, prevented them from making advances in most fields of knowledge. Their writing system remained simple and their pictographs elementary. If the true measure of a civilization is what it leaves behind, the Aztecs left no lasting legacy to compare with the ancient civilizations of Greece, Rome, or China.

COMMON ENGLISH WORDS DERIVED FROM THE AZTEC (NAHUATL) LANGUAGE

chicle	the priciple ingredient in chewing gum (giving its name to the common brand "Chiclets")
chili	a hot vegetable and spice
chocolate	derived from chocolatl, a drink made from the beans of the cacao tree
coyote	derived from coyotl, a member of the dog family
ocelot	derived from ocelotl, a member of the cat family similar to the jaguar
tomato	derived from tomatl

PART TWO: THE SPANISH CONQUEST

FINAL YEARS BEFORE THE CONQUEST

The Aztec world view was that of a past filled with natural and supernatural calamities. They continuously studied nature for portents about coming disasters: priests and magicians warned of coming times of tribulation, and the common people consulted fortune tellers regularly. The emperor at the time of the coming of the Spaniards, Moctezuma II, frequently consulted seers and wizards, and suffered troubling dreams prophesying a coming catastrophe. Moctezuma's mysticism and pessimism did little harm when these attitudes were shared by his enemies. When faced with a militarily superior invader, however, his state of mind did irreparable damage to the cause of his people.

For more than a decade before the arrival of the Spaniards, a series of events increased the sense of fatalism of the emperor and the people. These events, beginning with an eclipse of the sun in 1506 and followed by an earthquake, were seen as bad omens. In 1509 a terrifying "great comet," looking like a fire in the sky, appeared, and this was followed by a fire of mysterious origin at the top of the Great Temple pyramid, which burned the Great Temple down.

There were more earthquakes in 1512, and snow fell, which was extremely rare. The people of Tenochtitlán cried aloud in the streets and feared the coming of the end of the world. More sightings of comets and lightning bolts from the sky followed. A woman's voice was heard crying in the night in the streets of the capital, and she was taken to be the Snake-god mother weeping for the end of her children.

All this had a chilling effect on the deeply superstitious Moctezuma II. From about 1512 he began to have disturbing visions. He imagined two-headed men who disappeared as soon as he saw them. He saw a weeping woman with no flesh on her face. He also claimed to have seen a black smoking mirror set in the head of a strange crane-like bird caught in a net and brought to him for his examination. In this mirror he saw armed men on the backs of hornless deer. When he showed the bird to the priests, the vision had disappeared. Since any bearer of bad news was ritually murdered, Moctezuma feared the priests were lying to him about the coming disaster, and in his increasing madness he had their wives hanged and their children brutally killed by smashing their heads against a stone wall.

In an emperor-worshipping society such as that of the Aztecs, Moctezuma's fears were quickly sensed by the population, and fatalism and terror ran rampant. Aztecs greeted each other with tears of foreboding. The emperor felt that he was not appeasing the angry gods. As a result he followed policies that had disastrous results. Conquered peoples were taxed more heavily than ever in corn, jewels, and especially in victims for sacrifice. A new sacrificial stone was drenched in blood. The *pochteca* were ordered to surrender one-third of all their goods, and Aztec armies harassed subject people everywhere in the empire.

THE FIRST SIGNS OF THE SPANIARDS

One day a tired and crippled man arrived from the Gulf Coast and implored the guardians at the palace to allow him to speak to Moctezuma. The fact that this poor peasant had come on his own, putting his life in danger by even asking to speak to the emperor, gave him much credibility in the eyes of the Aztecs. He knelt before Moctezuma, asking forgiveness for his boldness, and said he had seen a great mountain on the waters floating from place to place without stopping. This mountain made noises like thunder. After throwing the man in prison, Moctezuma sent two trusted men to the coast to determine the veracity of the report. The men returned confirming the story and describing strange, ugly, short-haired, white-faced men with long beards who set out in a small boat from a winged "house on the water."

Further reports described how these men landed and fought with deadly grey swords harder and sharper than obsidian weapons. Riding on the backs of hornless deer, the men charged their enemies. More strangely, instead of whistling when they attacked, they shouted, and when victorious, they did not take victims for sacrifice. Their religious practices were even more bizarre, for they demanded that all human sacrifices should stop, and that people should pay homage to only one god. Instead of blood offerings to the gods, they insisted only flowers be brought to the image of a man hanging from a wooden cross.

It was the year 1518. In one of history's more remarkable coincidences, the sighting of this "mountain on the sea" coincided with the year *1 Reed* in the Aztec calendar, the end of a 52-year calendar cycle. It was also the year of Quetzalcoatl's birth, and the year of his prophesied return from the eastern sea. Moctezuma was convinced that the strange men were a sign of the return of this bearded, white-skinned god who had vanished centuries ago into the sea, vowing to return one day and reclaim his throne.

Reports arrived describing the leader of the newcomers, a pale-skinned man with a black beard, black tights, and black gloves. His colours, clothing, and jewelry, and especially his hat, resembled those of Quetzalcoatl. Moctezuma was more convinced than ever of the arrival of the god. He commissioned his finest artisans to make

Fig. 3.14
Upon hearing of the strange, bearded foreigners and their house on the sea, Moctezuma II and his advisers weep.

beautiful gifts for the strangers. After all, was this not the year of the end of a calendar cycle, with the possibility of another destruction of the world and its inhabitants? Perhaps, Moctezuma thought, he could forestall the inevitable with these gifts.

Of course the "mountain that moved in the sea" was a sixteenth century Spanish galleon, and the white, bearded men were Spaniards aspiring to reach the fabled El Dorado. This legend of a rumoured paradise in the Indies, with golden pebbles in the sea as large as bird's eggs, drove a restless and adventurous generation of Spaniards across the western sea to these new lands. Because land routes to Asia had been made unsafe by Turkish highwaymen, Europeans set out to find a water route to this storied land, and on the heels of voyages to the New World by Christopher Columbus, there was an explosion of men wanting to go to the land where they believed they could acquire riches. By the time the Aztecs sighted Hernando Cortés and his ships, the Spaniards already ruled Cuba and several other Carib-

bean islands, and were looking to expand farther west and south.

The exciting story of the Spanish Conquest of the Aztecs has been told and retold many times. It is an astonishing and spellbinding tale of how a tiny band of Spaniards under the bold Cortés made its way into the heart of the Aztec empire, captured Moctezuma, destroyed Tenochtitlán, and forced the Amerindian people to accept Spanish rule. The great empire of the Aztecs crumbled soon after the landing of the conquerors (known as conquistadores). Cortés cleverly divided the Amerindians, and by cajoling, threatening, and at times brutalizing them was able to use many of them to defeat Moctezuma's empire. (Cortés also had to deal with the resistance of his own men who, frightened and feeling isolated, frequently wanted to sail home; he had to burn their ships to prevent this from happening.)

Amerindian fighters were at a technological disadvantage when fighting the Spanish, who had horses and cannon. The Aztecs, used to fighting limited types of wars, were destroyed by an invader who practised total war and killed as many of the enemy as possible, rather than capturing them. Furthermore, these few hundred Spaniards were fighting an enemy who, weakened by superstition and fear, invited them into their capital city. Here the Aztec's empire was destroyed.

CORTÉS AND THE SPANIARDS

Hernando Cortés was born in 1485 into a poor but noble family in southern Spain. As

Fig. 3.15
The Spanish conquistadore Hernan Cortés,
conqueror of the Aztecs.

a young man, Cortés was impressed by stories of wealth and adventure in the New World so recently discovered by Columbus. He joined an expedition and reached America in 1504, where he settled on the Caribbean island of Santo Domingo. His ambitions, though, were much greater than that of a mere settler, and he had no intention of working the soil when there were rumours of gold to be had.

A ship returning from Yucatán filled with gold and silver led the governor of Santo Domingo to commission an expedition to the coast of the mainland, and Cortés was appointed a captain-general for the enterprise. The ships that sailed from Santo Domingo in 1518 carried 110 sailors, 553 soldiers, a few hundred menial labourers from the island's Amerindian population, sixteen horses, and a few cannon. This expedition marked the beginning of the downfall of an empire.

In a stroke of good luck, when the ships were at an island off the coast of Yucatán, a naked man rowed out to them. He claimed to be Jeronimo de Aguilar, a Spaniard who had been shipwrecked on the island years before, and he had learned the Mayan language. Cortés was later to add to his entourage an Amerindian woman who spoke both Mayan and the Aztec tongue of Nahuatl. The woman's name was Malinche, called Dona Mariña by the Spaniards, the daughter of an Aztec chief. She had been sold to the Maya as a slave, and her hatred for the Aztecs and reputed love for Cortés caused her to serve him loyally. She was an important source of information for Cortés about the empire of Moctezuma and abut the religious superstitions and legends of the long-lost god Quetzalcoatl. It was she who had dressed Cortés in black for the approach of Moctezuma's messengers. Later she was to have a son by him, Don Martin Cortés. Most importantly, through a three-way translation from Malinche to Aguilar to Cortés, the Spaniard would eventually be able to communicate with the Aztecs.

Exploring the coast of Mexico in 1519 while searching for lost members of an earlier expedition, the fleet stopped to drop anchor periodically for some local trade. On the coast of the Yucatán peninsula the Spaniards landed at the territory of the Tabascans, who had received a Spanish vessel on friendly terms the year before. This time the Tabascans resisted the Spanish landing, and the morning after the Spaniards had disembarked, the natives attacked. The Amerindians fought bravely and fiercely but the guns and horses helped the Spaniards to overcome them. Stories of the Spanish weapons that spat fire and of their huge, charging animals spread fear amongst neighbouring tribes.

Cortés next sailed to Vera Cruz. Reports of his arrival threw Moctezuma into a panic. The emperor commanded his best craftsmen, goldsmiths, and featherworkers to make gifts for the invaders, gifts suitable for the gods. Moctezuma's envoys brought to the Spaniards a shield fringed with quetzal feathers, jewelry of precious stones and metals, a book about the previous lives of Quetzalcoatl, and, most ominously for the Aztecs, gold and silver disks. It was these last items that piqued the interest of Cortés and his men. In exchange Cortés gave the Aztecs some glass trinkets and beads, and for good measure demonstrated his weaponry by shooting off a cannon. The messengers fainted, terrified at this evidence of thunder that caused waves and destroyed a tree onshore.

THE MARCH TO TENOCHTILÁN

Cortés began his march inland. At the Totonac city of Zempoala he gained a most important insight. Five Totonac chiefs complained to him about Aztec tax collectors and demands for tribute. They also informed the Spaniards that other tribes felt the same resentment, especially the fierce Tlaxcalans. The news that the Aztec empire was not a united one was valuable information. It was here also that Cortés and his men witnessed their first human sacrifice. Several Amerindians were ritually sacrificed each day by priests whose hair and robes were matted with blood. Angered, Cortés and his men overturned religious idols and demanded that the practice be stopped. His men cleaned and scrubbed the blood-spattered temple and placed a cross at the top. The Totonacs accepted conversion and became allies of the Spaniards.

Now aided by well over one thousand allies, Cortés decided to march into the Aztec empire through the valley inhabited by the Tlaxcalans, a tribe that had been left independent by the Aztecs as a source of victims for sacrifice. The Tlaxcalans did not trust anyone and were ready to fight on the least pretext. They at first attacked Cortés with an army that far outnumbered the Spaniards. The Spaniards and their horses were not gods to the Tlaxcalans and both were carved to pieces by sharp obsidian blades. The Spaniards finally overcame this bold but disorganized attack, and the Tlaxcalans, respecting the brave Spanish warriors, became valuable and loyal allies of Cortés.

Cortés was now summoned to Tenochtitlán by Moctezuma, who hoped to win him over from the Tlaxcalans. With 6000 new allies, Cortés began his march to the capital by way of Cholula where, through Malinche, he learned of a conspiracy against him by the warriors of the city. Cortés decided to use this situation to show his strength. He tricked the Cholulan chiefs into entering the temple courtyard, and had them all slaughtered by his soldiers and

Fig. 3.16
An ancient Aztec drawing shows a Spanish soldier leading his native allies against the Aztecs.

Amerindian allies. Thousands of Cholulans were killed, a message not lost on Moctezuma.

The advance to Tenochtitlán continued into October through snowy mountain passes. This journey involved great hardships. The road was a narrow footpath up and down the mountains. Rain and cold plagued the marchers. Along the way envoys from Moctezuma approached with food and greetings, but Malinche was suspicious of these men. The meat was seized and proved to be from human sacrifice.

Finally the Spaniards and their allies gazed down into a valley and saw a great city on a beautiful clear lake, with stone pyramids, canals, causeways, bridges, canoes, and dark red streams flowing down the temple steps. Many of the soldiers could not believe their eyes: here was a city of 200 000

people. The population of the Spanish city of Seville was only 45 000, that of Toledo only 18 000.

THE ENTRANCE OF THE SPANIARDS INTO TENOCHTITLÁN

What then took place must have been one of the great spectacles of history, the meeting of leaders from two different worlds. Moctezuma, carried by nobles on a litter decorated with green feathers, gold, silver, and pearls, was brought to meet Cortés. Beautiful tapestries were spread out in his path. Cortés dismounted, bowed, and presented a perfumed necklace made from glass beads, while Moctezuma placed necklaces of gold on his guests. The Spaniards were taken into the city and given quarters in the home of a former Aztec ruler. The soldiers were then given gifts, including two gold collars each, and this whetted their appetites for more treasure. (The Aztecs considered the passion of the Spaniards for gold passing strange, as they thought this metal to be the excrement of the gods.) Cortés was distrustful of this courteous welcome, and as a clever soldier, realized he was trapped inside an enemy city of more than 100 000 soldiers with only a few hundred men of his own. He commanded his men to keep constant guard.

What happened next further convinced him of the need for bold and dramatic action. After a few days, Cortés' men asked and were allowed to climb the stairway to the main temple. At the summit, in a gold-plated room with beautiful hangings caked with dried blood, they found three human hearts still warm and beating, dancing priests with blood-clotted hair, down to the ankles of some, and the stench of death. A skull rack gave them the feeling that soon their heads might be there, too. These sights increased the uneasy feeling the soldiers had that they were trapped in a barbaric city. Spanish morale was declining and rumours spread among them of an imminent Aztec attack.

Cortés assayed the situation and decided to make the first strike, believing that the Aztecs would submit to a captive emperor the same way Europeans would. On a pretext he had Moctezuma seized and taken prisoner. Moctezuma, in order to save face, told his people he was going of his own accord. Some Aztec officers were falsely charged with murdering some soldiers left at the Spanish garrison at Yucatán, and were burned alive at the stake, a previously unknown punishment to the Aztecs. This burning took place in front of the palace, for the population to see.

Moctezuma was held a prisoner, but in splendour, with two wives, and several personal servants. Spanish soldiers treated him with the deference owed an emperor and bowed and raised their hats when he passed. He in turn gave them chains of gold for their small kindnesses. He also gave Cortés great amounts of gold in hopes of peace, but the Spaniard continued to hold him prisoner. Cortés and Moctezuma met frequently, and Cortés promised that soon he would leave the kingdom with the tribute he had collected, and would only return once each year to collect more, in the Aztec manner. This unlikely situation continued for six months, with a tiny Spanish army holding hostage the head of the Aztec empire in the midst of his own crowded city, where the Spaniards could be trapped at any time.

THE DEATH OF MOCTEZUMA AND THE NOCHE TRISTE

That winter Cortés temporarily left Tenochtitlán for the coast in order to fight a Spanish army sent by the Spanish governor of Cuba, who had become jealous of his authority. This army apparently carried the smallpox virus to the mainland, an event that was to prove decisive in the conquest of the Aztecs and the Incas by killing countless thousands and destroying the agricultural labour force, leading to a famine that killed numberless more. In Tenochtitlán Cortés left behind 150 Spaniards under Pedro de Alvarado, a brave, cruel, and impetuous soldier. Alvarado believed that the Aztecs would be fools not to attack the Spanish garrison; as time passed his feelings of isolation grew. After giving permission for the Aztecs to celebrate a religious festival in the temple compound, Alvarado, seeing the great square outside the Spanish garrison filled with armed warriors, feared incorrectly that the celebration was being used to begin an attack. He saw this as a golden opportunity to destroy the cream of the Aztec fighting force, and Alvarado and his men blocked all the gates, attacked the Amerindians ferociously, and massacred them. The angered Aztec population of Tenochtitlán finally rose up in rebellion.

The Spanish soldiers were forced to take refuge in the garrison.

Cortés, greatly angered at Alvarado, returned to the silent and sullen city and entered the garrison. The next day wave after wave of whistling Aztec warriors under *Cuitlahuac*, Moctezuma's younger brother, attacked the Spaniards. The attackers were mowed down by shot but continued to attack until evening, when they withdrew. The attack continued the next day; captured Spaniards were dragged up the stairs of the temple to have their beating hearts cut out and offered to the sun.

When the Aztecs showed no signs of letting up on their attacks, Cortés went to Moctezuma and asked him to try and halt the attacks. Moctezuma, whether under duress or not is unclear, addressed the people from a rooftop and implored them to lift the siege and return home. What happened next is uncertain, as reports from chroniclers vary. Moctezuma was listened to with respect by some, but others now saw him as a traitor. He was hit by a rock and knocked unconscious to the ground, dying four days later. Some reports say he died from his wounds, others that the wounds were not serious and he committed suicide or was killed by the Spaniards. The besieged Spaniards then succeeded in a counterattack, sacked the Great Temple, and destroyed the idols. Cortés, in an attempt to restore order, tried to speak from the temple summit, but was hooted down.

The position of the beleaguered Spaniards was becoming desperate. Starving and short of water, many were dying and others were ill or wounded. Gunpowder was grow-

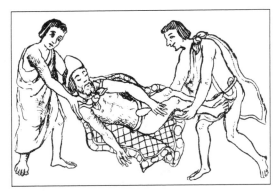

Fig. 3.17
The death of Moctezuma.

ing short. The Aztecs had burned all bridges and causeways leading out of Tenochtitlán to prevent Cortés and his men from escaping. Finally the Spaniards attempted to sneak away on the night of June 30, 1520, a night with no moon to light their escape, by using a portable wooden bridge.

The Aztecs detected their flight, sounded shell trumpets, and thousands of canoes came out on the lake to attack them. The wooden bridge collapsed, and the soldiers had to swim for their lives. Hundreds of soldiers, weighted down with as much silver and gold as they could pack into their armour, fell into the canal and drowned. Others were captured and sacrificed, but finally a bedraggled remnant, including Cortés, escaped. All the cannons were left behind, most of the horses were dead, 450 Spaniards were killed, and virtually all escapees were wounded. This night has come to be known as the *noche triste*, the "sad night" of retreat. Cortés is reputed to have wept under a tree for his fate and the fate of his men.

THE DESTRUCTION OF TENOCHTITLÁN

As Cortés retreated, Aztec soldiers pursued him. On an open field called Ocumba, tens of thousands of Amerindians from cities around the lake, the largest single force ever assembled in America, attacked the remnants of the Spanish forces. Left with no hope of retreat, a wounded Cortés and a group of horsemen charged a conspicuous, feather-clad chief who was carrying a gold banner. When this leader was wounded, the Aztecs ceased to fight, and retreated from what seemed certain victory. Cortés then went with his men to Tlaxcala to recover. Here he was joined by nearly a thousand well-armed Spanish reinforcements who had been landing periodically at the coast.

Six months after the *noche triste* Cortés and his army left Tlaxcala. During the next year he conquered all the cities loyal to the Aztecs, and prevented those cities from sending grain to Tenochtitlán, thus cutting the city's food supply in half.

By a brilliant stroke Cortés had his men build a fleet of thirteen **brigantines**, which were brought in sections across 100 km of rugged, almost vertical, mountain terrain from the coast and launched on Lake Texcoco. Tenochtitlán was placed under siege. Now no attack by Aztec canoes could have any chance of success. Nevertheless the Aztec warriors determined to fight to the bitter end, and the battle for Tenochtitlán was one of the bloodiest struggles for possession of a city in all history.

The Aztecs were finally waging war in the full realization that their opponents were not gods but men bent on destroying the Aztec way of life. An offer by Cortés of safety for the new emperor, Cuauhtemoc, was refused. Cuauhtemoc was no Moctezuma, and would not be a puppet. Cortés realized that if he was going to capture the city he would have to destroy it first. For 75 days bitter fighting took place. Twice during this time the Aztecs had the opportunity to slay Cortés, but left him alive with the intention of capturing him for sacrifice.

Under the Spanish siege people were barely subsisting on a diet of birds, lizards, grass, flowers, deer skins, even dirt. Many died from starvation. Towards the end of the siege Aztec children were dying of dysentery from drinking polluted water. Cannons knocked down walled defenses. Most resistance was finally crushed, with only one-eighth of the city left under Aztec control.

Finally, methodically destroying the city street by street, building by building, the Spaniards approached the city centre. Three-quarters of the buildings were levelled and the Great Temple pyramid was stormed. Here, in anger at finding the skulls and skin of some of their fellows being readied to be sent to other towns in order to prove the Spaniards were not gods, the invaders burned down the beautiful gilded cedar shrines. The few remaining warriors, weakened by smallpox and famine, still refused to surrender and so were slaughtered. The Aztecs who fled to neighbouring towns were killed by the citizens who for so long had suffered under Aztec rule. Every Spaniard was wounded, including Cortés; his men poured hot oil into their wounds to cauterize them.

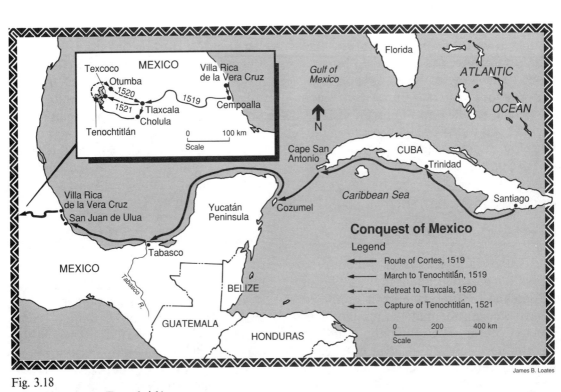

Fig. 3.18
Cortés' journey to Tenochtitlán.

Cortés had the rubble-strewn remains of the city burned. The Spaniards, a few surviving Aztec soldiers, and a handful of rescued civilians abandoned the razed remains of the once-great city. Nearly a quarter of a million Aztecs are estimated to have died during the siege of Tenochtitlán.

The last of the Aztec emperors, Cuauhtemoc, surrendered on August 13, 1521, while his city reeked with the stench of corpses and the river ran red with the blood of its citizens. Cuauhtemoc was tortured in an attempt to get him to reveal where more gold was hidden, but he refused to speak. His great character in the face of unspeakable tortures and the loss of his people has become legendary, and he is remembered as a great hero by Mexicans today. Three years after the fall of Tenochtitlán, he was hanged by Cortés.

The victory of the Spanish conquistadore Hernando Cortés must be ranked by any standard as a remarkable feat. In just over two years he and a handful of men, with the help of some Amerindians, mostly Totonacs and Tlaxcalans, destroyed an empire. Cortés was now named governor and captain-general of "New Spain of the Ocean Sea" and set about consolidating his rule. The remains of Tenochtitlán were levelled, the temple pyramid blown up, and a new Spanish city was built on top. Long-suffering tribes pledged allegiance to New Spain. Mining and shipbuilding were begun.

Cortés kept a promise he had made to Moctezuma to care for his children and had three royal princesses married to Spanish nobles. The King of Spain became concerned about Cortés gaining too much power, and recalled him to Spain in 1529, where he was welcomed with great honour. After four more voyages in the Pacific he died in Spain in 1547.

THE END OF AZTEC CIVILIZATION

In 1519, the year of the Spanish landing, the population of Amerindians in the Valley of Mexico and Central America is estimated to have been approximately 15 million. Before the century was out only 2 million Amerindians were left. A great number of people in Tenochtitlán had been infected with the smallpox virus in 1520, and thousands died painful and lingering deaths, while countless others were left blind or disfigured by the disease. The majority of natives during the next several decades were killed by still other diseases brought by the Europeans, such as measles, influenza, tuberculosis, and the common cold, to which the Amerindians had little or no immunity. War and famine also took a heavy toll. Many stopped having children because they would be doomed to a life of slavery. Some historians say multitudes died from demoralization and broken hearts as they saw their civilization and their way of life destroyed.

After the destruction of the Aztec empire, the Spaniards proceeded to conquer the rest of the region, including the remaining Maya. Amerindian religions and values were not tolerated by Spanish rulers or religious leaders. Cortés' army used torture on the Aztecs, partly in the belief that the natives were still hiding much gold. Other Amerindian tribes were not exempt from this reign of terror, and even the peoples who fought on the side of Cortés were not spared. The end result was the complete destruction of a city, a religion, and 3000 years of Mesoamerican civilization.

IMPORTANT DATES IN AZTEC HISTORY

12th Century — Aztecs leave their home in Azatlan and begin their wanderings

1325 — Aztecs settle on unwanted islands of Lake Texcoco and found Tenochtitlán

1424 — Birth of Aztec empire as surrounding peoples subdued by Aztec warfare

1481 — Calendar stone and great sacrificial stone carved

1487 — Dedication of Great Temple of Tenochtitlán, marked by orgy of human sacrifice

1503 — Moctezuma II elected great speaker (emperor)

1519 — Cortés lands at Yucatán on April 28, marches into Tenochtitlán on November 8

1520 — Death of Moctezuma II; smallpox plague hits citizens of Tenochtitlán

1521 to 1525 — Siege and destruction of Tenochtitlán; ruin of Aztec empire and civilization

HIGHLIGHTS

1. Sometime in the twelfth century a small

band of Amerindians, known to history as the Aztecs, left their home and migrated into the Valley of Mexico.

2. They finally settled in the vicinity of Lake Texcoco. Among the marshes and swamps of the lake, while scorned by neighbouring tribes, they founded a city, Tenochtitlán, which eventually became a great market and religious centre with a population estimated to have been somewhere around 200 000.

3. The Aztecs believed the sun needed human blood and human hearts sacrificed to it in order for it to rise each day and provide light and warmth to the earth. As a result, much of the religious life of the people centred around the practice of human sacrifice. It has been estimated that possibly 20 000 lives were taken in this ritual bloodletting each year.

4. One controversial theory suggests that this sacrifice was a cover for cannibalism, because of the Aztec need for protein in a part of the world where sources of protein were few. This thesis has been widely criticized but has generated much discussion.

5. The Aztec social classes were organized into a rigid caste of slaves, commoners, and nobles. There was also a merchant class and a warrior class, most honoured of all groups in a militaristic society such as that of the Aztecs. Above all castes were the emperor and other high government officials.

6. The Aztec economy had a strong agricultural base, with corn as the staple crop. Other produce included beans, squash, chili peppers, tomatoes, and other vegetables. Cacao was particularly valued for its taste and as a medium of exchange. An alcoholic drink called *pulque* seems to have been commonly consumed despite severe legal restrictions.

7. The Aztec state was a warrior state. Neighbouring tribes were subjugated and forced to pay tribute in the form of goods and human victims for sacrifice.

8. Writing and the calendar were not as advanced among the Aztecs as they were in the Mayan Classic Period. Writing in particular had not progressed beyond pictograph writing. There were numerous superstitions and legends surrounding the days of the calendar, particularly when the two different calendars used by the Aztecs coincided after a 52-year cycle.

9. Aztec children were taught roles proper to their sex in Aztec culture. Boys were trained to be warriors; girls were raised to cook, weave, and carry out other domestic chores. Males had dominant roles in the society. Polygamy was allowed for men but not for women.

10. About the middle of the fifteenth century the Aztecs suffered a series of natural disasters that convinced them that the sun needed more blood than ever, and after this the incidence of sacrifice increased markedly.

11. Aztec society was both fatalistic and pessimistic about the future. Around the end of one of the calendar cycles the emperor Moctezuma II was told by a poor peasant about a great mountain floating on the ocean, with bearded, white-skinned men. He took this to be

the return of the god Quetzalcoatl, and tried to placate him with gifts and hospitality.

12. The ships were Spanish warships and the men were Spanish explorers, led by the great conquistadore Cortés. The Spanish used the disunity of the empire to destroy the city of Tenochtitlán and eradicate Aztec culture.

13. In less than a century following the fall of Tenochtitlán, the population of Amerindians in Mexico and Central America declined from some 15 million to 2 million people. Some died from starvation; many were killed in warfare; the majority died from the introduction of diseases unknown previously in America and to which the Aztecs had little immunity.

TERMS TO UNDERSTAND

Write a one-sentence explanation of each of the following terms. Write a sentence using each term.

brigantine
caste system
chinampas
conquistadores
demigod
flower wars
herbivorous animals
macehuelli
pictograph writing
pilli
pulque
scribes
teocalli
socialization
tlalcotli

DEVELOPING CRITICAL THINKING ABOUT CONCEPTS IN THE SOCIAL SCIENCES FOR INDIVIDUAL OR GROUP PRESENTATION

1. *EFFECTS OF ORIGINS*: What effects do the origins of peoples and nations have on their behaviour? How did the humble and low beginnings and unhappy experiences of the Aztecs effect their behaviour and actions once in power? What has been the effect of the way in which Canada began as a nation? Draw conclusions about the effects of early experiences upon national behaviour.

2. *EVALUATING HYPOTHESES*: What do you think of Harner's hypothesis about Aztec human sacrifice? Is it convincing? What are its strengths as a hypothesis and what are its weaknesses? Develop a hypothesis about some aspect of the Aztec world, for example, the reasons for such a strict upbringing of children, or the causes of the Aztec downfall.

3. *CASTE SYSTEMS*: Why do you think the Aztecs developed a system of classes such as that described in the chapter? What might have been its strengths and weaknesses? Describe the class system of our country and compare it with that of the Aztecs. Is our system rigid? Explain.

4. *MILITARISTIC CULTURES*: The Aztecs were a militaristic society dominated by warriors and warfare. What

other societies in history have been militaristic? What are the good and bad points about living in such a society? Compare Canada's degree of militarism in everyday life with that of another society, today or in the past, with which you are familiar.

5. *ORAL TRADITIONS*: Many societies pass legends, fables, and family history down through the generations by word of mouth. What are examples in our culture of such information? What other societies, today or in the past, have used an oral tradition? Give examples.

6. *SOCIALIZATION OF CHILDREN*: Why is it necessary for societies to socialize their children? In what ways does Canadian society socialize its children? Give specific examples.

7. *POLYGAMY*: Research other societies where polygamy has been legal, for example the Mormons of nineteenth century America. What was the rationale for allowing this practice? Why did it end in most places in this century?

8. *DEATH AND BURIAL CUSTOMS*: All societies have customs surrounding death and burial. Describe the burial customs of your culture or religion. Research its origins. Interview someone from a different culture or religion about burial customs in their community.

9. *THE EFFECTS OF DISEASE ON HISTORY*: Some historians believe that the role of disease has been underestimated as a force in history. Research and report on such plagues as the Black Death, the influenza epidemic following World War I, and other epidemics. An excellent resource for this subject is *Plagues and Peoples*, by William H. McNeill.

RELATED TOPICS FOR RESEARCH AND PRESENTATION

Aztec codices
Theories about human sacrifice
The Aztec calendar
The National Museum of Anthropology in Mexico City
Archaeological finds at Tenochtitlán
Moctezuma II
The Spanish invasion and Hernan Cortés

FOR ADDITIONAL READING AND RESEARCH

MAGAZINE AND JOURNAL ARTICLES

Note: The December 1980 National Geographic magazine has four excellent articles on the Aztecs; these are a good introduction for the interested high school student.

The articles are as follows:
"The Aztecs," Bart McDowell
"Building of Tenochtitlán," A. F. Molina Montes
"The Great Temple of Tenochtitlán," E. M. Moctezuma
"New Finds in the Great Temple," E. M. Moctezuma
Articles of interest from other journals are:

"Culture as Protein and Profit, Views of M. Harner on Human Sacrifice and Cannibalism of the Aztecs," *New York Review of Books*, November 23, 1978.

"The Enigma of Aztec Sacrifice," Michael Harner, *Natural History*, April, 1977.

"Grave findings at Ancient Mexican Site," (Teotihuacan), B. Bower, *Science News*, December 17, 1988.

"Poetry, Serpents, and Sacrifice," F. Golden, *Time Magazine*, August, 16, 1982.

"Why Were the Aztecs and Mayas Stuck in the Stone Age? Obsidian, a Kind of Volcanic Glass May be the Answer," T. Stocker, *Earth Science*, Summer, 1987.

BOOKS

Berdan F. F., *The Aztecs of Central Mexico: An Imperial Society.* Holt, Rinehart and Winston, New York, 1982.

Blacker, Irwin R., *Cortés and the Aztec Conquest.* American Heritage Publishing, New York, 1965.

Broda, Johanna, David Carrasco, and Eduardo Matos Moctezuma, *The Great Temple of Tenochtitlán, Center and Periphery of the Aztec World.* University of California Press, Berkeley, 1987.

Brundage, Burr C., *The Jade Steps, a Ritual Life of the Aztecs.* University of Utah Press, Salt Lake City, Utah, 1985.

Burland, C. A., *Montezuma.* G. P. Putnam's Sons, New York, 1973.

Castillo, Bernal Diaz Del, *The Discovery and Conquest of Mexico, 1517-1521.* Octagon Books, New York, 1970.

Coe, Michael D., *Mexico.* Third Edition, Thames and Hudson, New York, 1984.

Conrad, G. W., and A. A. Demarest, *Religion and Empire: The Dynamics of Aztec and Inca Expansionism.* Cambridge University Press, Cambridge, 1984.

Fagan, Brian M. *The Aztecs.* Freemen Press, New York, 1984.

Fehrenbach, T. R., *Fire and Blood, a Bold and Definitive Modern Chronicle of Mexico.* Bonanza Books, New York, 1973.

von Hagen, Victor Wolfgang, *The Aztecs: Man and Tribe.* Mentor Books, New American Library, New York, 1961.

Innes, Hammond, *The Conquistadores.* Collins, London, 1969.

Keen, Benjamin, *The Aztec Image in Western Thought.* Rutgers University Press, New Brunswik, New Jersey, 1971.

McNeill, William H., *Plagues and Peoples.* Doubleday/Anchor Press, Garden City, New York, 1971.

Pasztory, Esther, *Aztec Art.* Harry N. Abrams, New York, 1983.

Prescott, William H., *History of the Conquest of Mexico and History of the Conquest of Peru.* Random House, New York.

Sagahun, Fray Bernadino De, *Florentine Codex: General History of the Things of New Spain.* University of Utah and The School of American Research, translation published 1969.

Stuart, Gene S., *The Mighty Aztecs.* National Geographic Society, Special Publications, Washington D.C., 1981.

CHAPTER FOUR

THE INCAS

The great Inca civilization was virtually unknown beyond the borders of its empire. It stretched from today's central Chile in the south, through the Andes highlands of Bolivia and Peru, to northern Ecuador and southern Columbia in the north. This was a phenomenal area, nearly 5000 km in length, and varying in width from 160 to 650 km. This magnificent civilization, rivalling in size the greatest empires in the history of the world, collapsed quickly under the onslaught of Francisco Pizarro and his handful of Spanish conquistadores.

INTRODUCTION

Who were the Incas? What was their origin and how did they come to conquer and dominate such a vast area? Archaeologists who study the Inca empire have some advantages over those who study the Maya. The Mayan civilization was long dead by the time of Cortés and the Spanish invasion; the Incas were still flourishing at the time of the Spanish arrival. There are many eyewitness accounts from Spanish chroniclers of the greatness of this civilization. These chroniclers, including priests, soldiers, and even the **mestizo** (half Spaniard, half Amerindian) son of a conquistadore and an Inca princess, left books on Inca life and culture that still fascinate the reader. As always, however, such accounts must be weighed carefully, as they were written by invaders and conquerors with a tendency to romanticize their own exploits.

Unlike the Maya, the Incas had no written language. Aside from the Spanish accounts, what knowledge we have of the Inca and the people they conquered is derived from the huge numbers of artifacts they left behind. These include tapestries, textiles, stonework, metalwork, pottery, and knotted cords, called *quipu*, used to keep numerical data.

In recent years archaeologists have un-

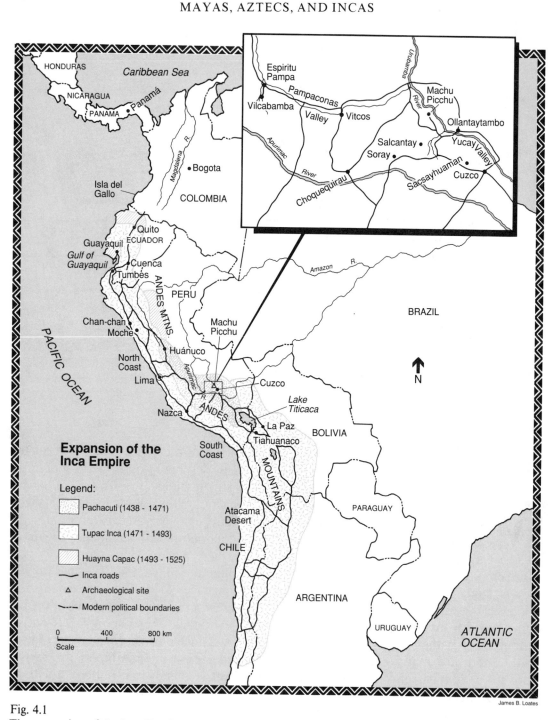

Fig. 4.1
The expansion of the Inca Empire

James B. Loates

covered similar artifacts from dozens of different pre-Inca peoples, speaking as many different languages, and living in the region that eventually became the Inca empire. These artifacts indicate a clear pattern of development in the Andean area, from the first simple hunting, gathering, and fishing communities to the eventual formation of local cultures with distinctive arts and crafts. Later some of these local cultures achieved high levels of civilization, such as the Chimú and Moche of the Andean north, the Nazca of the coastal south, and the Tiahuanaco on the shores of Lake Titicaca. It was the organizational genius of the Inca to amalgamate the diverse Amerindian people of this vast area into one empire.

PART ONE: PRE-INCA PERU

The Inca are the best known of all the Andean peoples, because of their domination of the Andes area at the time of the Spanish arrival. By then they had imposed their way of life, and especially their language, *Quechua*, on the many peoples in their empire. As they had no written language, their historians relied on an oral tradition that ignored the accomplishments and even the existence of earlier cultures. Any pre-Inca history to these "historians" was simply not important enough to be handed down.

With the birth of modern archaeology, the pre-Inca record and the importance of earlier civilizations have gradually come into focus. Peru and the surrounding Andean countries contain a rich trove of artifacts from these earlier peoples, preserved by the very dry and warm climate of the Peruvian coastal plain. Shell **middens**, huge mounds of the shells of mussels and crustaceans, discarded by the people who ate the seafood, have been found all along the coast of Peru at the most ancient sites. Sharp tools and weapons found in these middens indicate a hunting and fishing economy. There is as well evidence of simple cultivation of beans, cotton, and gourds. In later millennia this subsistence economy was augmented by the introduction of fish hooks and nets.

Three significant advances took place in the second millennium B.C.E., the introduction of pottery, the cultivation of maize, and the beginnings of stonework buildings. Possibly the most important advance occurred at Chavín de Huantar about 800 B.C.E. with the building of a sophisticated temple complex by a group whose actual name has yet to be learned, but who are referred to as the Chavín people.

THE CHAVÍN

Chavín culture was not identified by archaeologists until the 1920s. It is now clear that it was the first great Andean civilization, lasting six centuries dating from approximately 1000 B.C.E., and roughly paralleling the Olmec domination of Mexico. These Peruvian people built their huge ceremonial centres in the northern highlands. Pilgrims came long distances to them for religious ceremonies and sacrifices. It is also thought possible that they came to hear oracles predict the future. As excavations continue at Chavín de Huantar it is becoming clear that this centre remained an important site for magic and sorcery up to the Spanish conquest in the sixteenth century, long after the disappearance of the civilization that built it.

Although the Chavín culture had no form of writing, it was highly advanced in architecture and engineering, and its religious ideas extended far beyond its borders. Chavín social organization was advanced enough to be able to deploy great battalions of people for the construction of temples and other public works.

Archaeological evidence supports the contention that Chavín culture influenced most of what is modern Peru for most of the first millennium B.C.E. This period was by all evidence a peaceful one, a time when agricultural communities were developing. There is no evidence of arms, fortifications, or warfare at this time. The people seem to have been regularly involved with preparations for and participation in elaborate sacrificial feasts, with acrobatic folk dancing in colourful costumes, and folk music from reed instruments, accompanied by ample supplies of the sweet fermented corn drink called *chicha*.

This period of peaceful progress came to an end around 200 B.C.E., although the precise date is unknown. Archaeologists speculate that a natural disaster, such as an earthquake or flood, may have destroyed farms and temples, undermining the people's religious faith. Interestingly, this happened at about the same time as the decline of the Olmecs in Mesoamerica, a people with a similar religious system to the Chavín. Some experts have speculated upon the possible influence of Mexico and the Olmecs on Chavín culture, citing a similar religious belief in a man-jaguar god, and as well, some stylistic similarities in religious decoration. Others cite as arguments against such influence the great distances between the two areas and the lack of any similar cultures in the area between Mexico and Peru.

The people of Chavín de Huantar made significant cultural advances beyond those of earlier tribal groups. Unless and until conflicting evidence is found, they may be considered the precursors of the advanced civilizations that followed. Archaeological discoveries at their main ceremonial site of Chavín de Huantar are continuing to shed new light on this important early civilization and its deities. There are thousands of artifacts under the soil of Peru waiting to supply the answers to the riddles of this lost civilization.

THE NAZCAS

After the end of the Chavín predominance there followed more than a millennium of development of different cultures in different geographical regions of Peru. Progress was made during this period in agriculture, especially in irrigation and in fertilization with sea bird manure, called *guano*. Populations grew in these prosperous times, and cities and civilizations expanded. The two most important of the local cultures during this period were the Nazca of the south and the Moche of the north.

The Nazca people of the Pacific coast of southern Peru left a fascinating and baffling legacy that continues to intrigue experts and non-experts alike. This consists of a series of

Fig. 4.2
The Nazca drew eighteen bird shapes, ranging in
size from 30 to 300 m·long, across the desert
between the Andes Mountains and the Pacific
Ocean. The purpose of these desert drawings is
still a mystery.

more than 100 huge drawings of birds, animals, and geometric shapes and patterns of
crossing lines stretching across the desert of
this region. These drawings look as though
they were drawn by some giant hand and
are outlined by two rows of pebbles parallel
to each other. They were laid out some 1500
years ago, and since almost no rain has
fallen in this region for 1500 years, the pebbles remain undisturbed in their original
designs. The figures and patterns cannot be
seen from eye level; they can only be dis-
cerned from the air. The Spanish chroniclers do not mention their existence, and
they were not rediscovered until the modern era of aviation.

Some authors have imagined that these
drawings could only be the work of extra-
terrestial beings. More scientific explanations are no less fascinating. For many decades a German astronomer named Maria
Reiche has painstakingly studied and recorded these drawings, often while strapped
to the bottom of a light plane, and has suggested that the Nazca used scale model
drawings. They therefore could work out
their gigantic designs without the need for
an aerial view. By digging posts and stretching strings between them they were able to
make the lines straight.

For many years sightseers and the curious
walked upon and drove over the lines, causing much damage. Today the danger of the
drawings being ruined by sightseers has diminished now that, after much campaign-
ing for their preservation by Maria Reiche,
the government of Peru has declared the
area an archaeological zone and has banned
walking and driving over it.

Some who have studied the drawings
have speculated about astronomical meanings or magical uses for the lines. Other
observers have even gone so far as to pro-
pose that the Nazcas had the ability to make
a lighter-than-air craft with materials available to them such as vegetable fibre and
reeds. No explanation yet proposed is entirely satisfactory, and the Nazca lines remain one of the most intriguing puzzles
ever constructed.

THE MOCHE

Contemporary with the Nazca culture of
the south of Peru was the Moche, sometimes called Mochica, culture of the north.
The people of this culture built huge stone
pyramids, but were also able to produce
delicate portrait vases, textiles, jewelry, and
ceramics. Their artwork is considered to be

of great beauty, and in particular their gold-work indicates a high degree of metalworking ability. They dominated the north from approximately 200 to 600 C.E., before vanishing mysteriously.

Little is known about the Moche empire. It never developed a written language, its spoken language, *yunga*, has disappeared, and there is much disagreement among experts on how to interpret the figures on the Moche painted pottery. It seems that the idea of a caste system of ruling families containing superior human beings and working families made up of ordinary mortals was widely accepted in the society.

One of the most spectacular finds in the history of pre-Columbian archaeology occurred along the coast of Peru in 1987. Local police had raided the homes of Peru's "tomb looters," local citizens who dig for artifacts and sell them on the black market. These artifacts are ultimately destined for purchase by wealthy collectors in North America and Europe. Part of the police haul was a tiny ceramic piece with a small gold head, identified by Peruvian archaeologist Walter Alva as being over 1200 years old. The looters, after being promised that they would be hired on a dig, showed Alva the source of their find at the town of Sipan. Here Alva found a spectacular 1500-year old tomb from the Moche culture.

The first artifact found in the tomb was a wooden coffin, the first wooden coffin to be found in pre-Columbian America. The most important find of all, however, was the skeleton of a young warrior-priest covered from head to toe in gold, silver, and jewelled ornaments. He was buried wearing a turquoise bracelet, a copper headdress, and a five-kilogram solid gold cape. He carried a gold rattle decorated with an exquisite picture of a warrior beating a prisoner. Both his feet had been severed, and Alva speculates this may have been done to keep him at his guardpost in the after-life. The young soldier had been buried with two men, possibly servants, and two young women, likely wives or concubines. The remains of sacrificial llamas were also found.

In a race with the looters, Alva began a major excavation in 1988, partly financed by the National Geographic Society, in the hopes that by uncovering more such finds, the riddles of Moche culture may be solved. Already he has found thousands of vases, figurines, and bowls buried in the nearby area, and this site may rival the Mayan city of Palenque as one of the richest burial sites in all of the Americas.

TIAHUANACO

High in the Andes Mountains, on a barren plateau near the Bolivian shore of Lake Titicaca, lie the remains of an ancient, long-forgotten civilization. The remains are those of the city of Tiahuanaco, in fact the remains of five separate cities that flourished at this site, each city rising on the ruins of the previous one. This site was in use for nearly thirty centuries, from 1500 B.C.E. to 1200 C.E., with the peak of its influence from 450 to 900 C.E. At the height of their power the Tiahuanacans eliminated the Moche and Nazca cultures and ruled over all Peru. Like so much else about this culture, how this was accomplished is unknown, as the archaeological record does not indicate whether dominion was achieved by conquest or through more peaceful means.

By the time of the Spanish arrival the city was long uninhabited, most of its handsome stones having been removed for building materials. The Amerindians who brought sacrifices to the giant statues told the Spaniards that the Incas had come to the area in the fifteenth century and found it already abandoned. These Amerindians spoke of demons having built the site. What was left by this time were huge stone gateways opening on to emptiness, and giant statues that stood alone against the sky. This is how Tiahuanaco appears today. Because of its enormous size and haunting grandeur, the site has excited the imagination of many observers, some of whom have concluded that only a race of giants or spacemen could have worked with stones so huge.

The Tiahuanacans controlled an area greater than anyone else up to that time in American history. In fact it has been said that the Incas carried on from where the Tiahuanacans left off, although the Tiahuanacans vanished so suddenly and completely that the Incas, surveying their ruins, thought they were the ruins of a far more ancient site.

Like other Andean peoples, the inhabitants of Tiahuanaco kept no written records. What pictures remain in the form of carved stone are undeciphered, and it is unclear whether or not they represent actual picture writing. The results of one hundred years of archaeological digging have shed little light on this important but mysterious site. Archaeologists have found over the years that it is wise to listen carefully to local legends about a site, as investigation

often reveals that they are based in fact. The Amerindian fishermen on Lake Titicaca spoke to some archaeologists of sunken palaces in the lake, whose roofs touched the bottom of their boats during dry periods. Despite the risk of using an aqualung at high altitudes, underwater archaeologists discovered buried walls covered in slime, and wharves for ships. The purposes of these constructions have yet to be determined.

Aerial photography has revealed a circle of suburbs that has caused experts to reassess their original thesis that Tiahuanaco was only a religious site. These suburban buildings could not be seen from ground level as they were not made from stone but from dried mud, and had crumbled into dust that looked like the surrounding soil. It now seems clear that there was once a city on the site, and that the population of the suburbs included craftsmen such as metalworkers, potters, and weavers.

The most perplexing of all questions is how the giant stones, some with a mass of up to one hundred tonnes, reached a site located at such a high altitude. No rock quarries or other sources of building materials are nearby, and the method used to transport the stones is a mystery. Speculation focuses on the enormous number of workers that had to have been available to move heavy stones, using ropes made from llama skin. The roads would be terraced for frequent rests, and it is estimated by some that it may have taken 50 to 60 years to move some of the larger stones.

Still, the problem of how the stones were moved past natural obstacles has never been satisfactorily resolved; it must be kept in mind that, like other Amerindians, the

Fig. 4.3
This huge stone Tiahuanacan gateway was carved from a single rock; it now opens on a barren plain. The drawings on the gateway are thus far indecipherable.

Tiahuanacans never knew the use of the wheel. The construction of Tiahuanaco, the purpose for which it was built, the people who inhabited it, and the reason it was abandoned all remain a mystery.

THE CHIMÚ

In the twelfth century C.E. the Chimú civilization built a great city at Chan Chan, on the Peruvian coast just inland from the Pacific Ocean. Here the Moche River was used to irrigate the fields surrounding the city.

The Chimú forged an empire that would be the second most extensive and powerful ever to exist in pre-Columbian South America. Chimú culture was organized in a rigid caste system dominated by an aristocracy made up of about ten per cent of the population. Members of the aristocracy were, like those of the Moche, considered superior to the rest of the population. The lower tier of this rigid society was made up of hard-working builders and artisans who lived in poor neighbourhoods with windowless houses. The ruling aristocracy of this largest city of all in pre-Columbian America lived in luxury behind high-walled compounds in buildings made of **adobe** (sun-dried bricks made form unfired clay).

When a ruler died, an elaborate ceremony was held during which his body, together with his gold and silver, was placed inside his compound. This ceremony included the sacrifice of scores of young women, whether willingly or unwillingly is unclear, to join him in the next life. His compound was then enclosed and sealed. At the same time the new ruler began to build his compound. As generation followed generation, the city became a place for the dead and their gold.

The Chimú produced beautiful goldwork, jewelry, and ceramics. Their textiles and tapestries have rarely been surpassed at any time in world history. Male and female weavers would toil for years on one work, using advanced loom techniques, a wide array of vegetable and mineral dyes that have still not faded, and excellent quality llama, alpaca, and vicuña wool. Cotton was also used, and as this was one of the rare plants common to both the Old and the New World, a comparison of the contemporary tapestries can be made. European and Asian tapestries used about 40 threads per centimetre, the Chimú used about 100. Spanish explorers looted and melted down much Chimú goldwork; but their interest in tapestries was minimal and this, along with the dry Peruvian climate, has allowed many beautiful works to survive and testify to the greatness of Chimú weavers.

A society's laws can reveal a great deal about that society; punishments for crimes can tell us much about the values of a culture. In the Chimú culture the rigidity of the caste system was paramount, and therefore any crime against it was severely, even brutally, punished: the criminal was buried alive with the bones of other criminals or animals. Theft was frowned upon in this property-conscious society, and a captured thief, as well as his father and brothers, was executed by the victim of the theft.

The Chimú empire collapsed quickly when invaded by the Incas, perhaps because the lower caste may have felt little motivation to defend such a cruel regime.

FROM PRE-INCA CIVILIZATIONS TO THE INCAS

All these pre-Inca peoples farmed either the high **sierra** (a long, jagged chain of mountains) or the coastal valleys, using great irrigation canals and extensive fertilization. They were all adept at weaving wool from the llama, alpaca, guanaco, and vicuña, and each excelled at metallurgy, particularly with gold and silver. They were expert stonemasons, the size of the stone seemingly no problem. In the deserts where stone was unavailable they worked as expertly with adobe, and today after so many centuries one can still see remains of their sun-baked brickwork.

Most of these cultures had kings who had both religious and secular powers. The most important god seems to have been a creator-god, often called Viracocha, a Tiahuanacan name, although there were many other gods in control of the forces of nature. The sun was the supreme power, and there were often ceremonies of human sacrifice. Viracocha, like the Aztec god Quetzalcoatl, was reputed to have promised to return to his people one day.

When the Tiahuanaco civilization collapsed, the cities disappeared and people lived in villages and on farms, and followed more ancient customs. Possibly the re-emergence of tribal loyalties led to rebellions and the break-up of empires into smaller tribes. All of these tribes, from the most advanced to the simplest, were conquered by the Incas, who emerged from their midst and who absorbed them into the Inca empire. The languages of these tribes disappeared, and cultural distinctions were lost in the blending of a new Inca culture.

What distinguished the Incas from their predecessors was their great ambition and their pragmatic ability to copy the best ideas of others. A comparison between the Incas and the Romans is instructive. Both were very adept at the practical as opposed to the artistic. Both were temperamentally prepared to borrow much of their culture, the Incas from the pre-Inca peoples discussed above, the Romans from the Greeks and Egyptians. Both, then, were superb adaptors of the ideas of others, not hesitating to assimilate ideas and art forms as well as conquered people within their empire.

PART TWO: THE EMPIRE OF THE INCAS

EARLY HISTORY

The emergence of the Incas in the central Andes Mountains cannot be precisely dated, but seems to have occurred somewhere between the years 1100 and 1200 C.E.

The Inca had their own myths about their origins. Early Spanish chroniclers told of the Inca legends of four brothers and four sisters leaving a cave somewhere south of Cuzco, called "Tavern of the Dawn," and leading groups called *ayllus* in search of arable land. After several years one man, Manco Capac, killed his three brothers, and along with his sisters and other survivors came to the valley of Cuzco. Here they forced out the inhabitants, and settled to found a city, Cuzco, that would be the centre of their empire, with Manco Capac as the first Inca. The term Inca commonly refers both to the name of the people and the title of the head of the people, as in "the Inca."

Other competing myths were handed down orally by the Inca and were later recorded with questionable accuracy by the Spanish chroniclers. One of these is the legend of the "Golden Wedge." According to this story, the sun sent to the shores of Lake Titicaca a male child and a female child who were to civilize the sun's wayward children of the earth. They were directed by the sun to carry a "golden wedge" and to settle where it sank on its own. The wedge sank and disappeared at Cuzco. The children travelled to the north and south to spread the news of their successful mission from the sun. A new kingdom was born where the sun's daughter taught the women civilized female living on the Inca model, and the son taught the men how to fight. All succeeding Incas descended from this pair, according to this legend. The story was probably concocted late in Inca history in order to legitimize the Inca royal family as having a godlike origin.

The Inca originated in the Cuzco area and not in the Lake Titicaca basin as this legend claimed. If the Inca had originated in the area of Lake Titicaca, they could claim to be descended from the great civilization at Tiahuanaco. But their northern origin is borne out by archaeological evidence and by the similarities of the Inca language to others in the Cuzco region.

The early history of the high valley of Cuzco is a history of fighting, raiding, and feuding among the various peoples in the region. These peoples shared a common culture and language, and had a similar physical appearance (dark brown skin and squat, stocky build). The Incas were simply one of these peoples, but during the twelfth century they emerged as the dominant group, probably because of their superior social organization.

For more than a century after this time the Incas seemed content to be the most prestigious tribe in the valley, but about the year 1438, under the great Inca *Pachacuti*, a period of conquest began. This quest for empire continued and the Inca domain grew ever larger until the Spanish arrival in 1530 ended the era of Inca domination.

Fig. 4.4
A Spanish drawing of the Inca Pachacuti

THE EXPANSION OF THE INCA EMPIRE

Sixteenth century Incas could recite a list of their thirteen past emperors, starting with the semi-legendary Manco Capac and ending with Atahualpa, executed by the conquistadore Pizarro in 1533. It is commonly considered that Pachacuti ("he who remakes the world"), the ninth Inca, was the greatest of Inca rulers, and indeed he is viewed by some historians as the most illustrious of all Amerindian leaders at any time in history.

Before Pachacuti the Incas were just another of the dozens of tribes of the Andes Mountains. It is Pachacuti who made the Andes Mountains an Inca preserve, and it was he who built the Inca capital at Cuzco as the centre of a great empire. He is also given credit for developing the Inca religion and

117

system of government. To his people he was a leader of enormous stature whose sayings were repeated as wisdom and whose conquests took his people to greatness. He ruled from 1438 to 1471; during his rule he set the pattern for the remainder of the Inca period by assimilating conquered populations into the Inca system. He did this by breaking them up and relocating them in Inca areas where they had to adopt the Inca language, laws, and customs.

Pachacuti's son Tupa Inca Yupanqui, the equal of his father as a military leader, continued his father's policies by becoming one of the greatest conquerors in all of history. In territory conquered he rivalled both Alexander the Great and Napoleon. His rule lasted from 1471 to 1493, and under his leadership the empire expanded to its southern-most extent into Chile. The process of assimilating conquered tribes was perfected, with a policy of firmness, and, when necessary, cruelty. During the reigns of this father and son the great fortresses at Sacsayhuaman and Machu Picchu were built to further buttress the empire against any threat.

The third great leader of this triumvirate of Inca conquerors was Pachacuti's grandson and Tupa Inca's son Huayna Capac, who ruled from 1493 to 1525. He moved the empire northwards into what is today Ecuador and Colombia. Here he settled in Quito, making it the capital of an empire equal in extent to the Roman empire at its peak, and here he remained, unaware of the presence of Columbus and the onrushing Spaniards. This was the high water mark of the Inca empire, for after the death of Huayna Capac there ensued a struggle for power among his sons. This disunity occurred at the precise time when the Inca empire was facing its greatest threat from the Spanish.

INCA WARFARE AND CONQUEST

Centuries of living in the high Andes had given the Inca enlarged lungs, enabling them to breathe the thin mountain air comfortably. Their initial conquests were in the mountains, where their stamina worked to their benefit. Having gained control of the mountain passes and the valleys below, they marched to the coast where they surrounded and defeated the remnants of the Chimú kingdom, gaining control of Chan Chan and other cities. They then moved south. Although some valley tribes submitted without a struggle, others fought bitterly. Finally by 1493 the Incas had conquered a greater empire than either the Chavín or the Tiahuanacans at the peak of their rule.

Inca warriors fought barefoot, wearing a short tunic, using a wooden shield, and wearing a wooden or metal helmet. They used clubs and axes with sharp stone blades. Soldiers were equipped with headbands that they could unloosen to use as a slingshot, a weapon of great popularity. The Inca fighting methods were not outstanding. It was a genius for organization that made the Inca superior to their enemies. This genius showed in their superb lines of supply and communication.

The Inca preferred to have the enemy surrender peacefully rather than fight. And in time the Inca fighting reputation grew such that neighbouring tribes frequently conceded defeat before battle and negotiated a peaceful capitulation, realizing that resistance was hopeless and would only cause unnecessary bloodshed. The Inca military was usually exemplary in its behaviour towards the conquered, rarely engaging in violent acts of revenge or brutality. (They were, however, known to make flutes out of the thigh bones of their victims.)

During the century of its predominance, the Inca empire was highly unified compared with other empires in history. The process of **mitima**, or forced colonization, begun by Pachacuti, uprooted potential troublemakers from the conquered peoples and transplanted them amongst loyal and faithful Inca or Inca followers. Their place among their own people was taken by previous *mitimaes* who had long been under Inca rule and were no longer viewed as a possible source of opposition.

The nobility of the conquered peoples were also broken up and relocated, and the defeated chief and his sons were brought to Cuzco. Here they were treated as visiting royalty, even if they were visiting by compulsion. Their idols were brought to the royal court and were worshipped alongside Inca idols. Tribal chiefs were taken into the Inca fold by immersing them in Inca ways. They were also forced to learn and use the Inca language. This was all preparation for their eventual return to their own people, to rule as local representatives and loyal subjects of the Inca.

When the conquered chief, now an Inca follower, was allowed to go home, his eldest son stayed behind at the royal court as hostage for his father's good behaviour. All laws of the conquered tribe that did not contradict Inca laws were retained, and the conquered subjects were made citizens of equal standing in the Inca realm. Any sign of rebellion was ruthlessly suppressed by breaking up the community. Those perceived as disloyal were deported to take their place among the loyal elsewhere. In time a conquered tribe was indistinguishable from an older Inca community, and by the close of the fifteenth century rule from Cuzco was unquestioned over a large area stretching from southern Colombia to central Chile, incorporating probably hundreds of diverse peoples.

THE AYLLU

The **ayllu**, or clan of extended families, was the basic social unit of Inca society, and each Inca was born into one. The *ayllu* probably derived from the traditional family or kin group of pre-Inca times, which was the basic unit for land ownership and local government. Each *ayllu* believed that all of its members were descended from a common ancestor, and intermarriage within the group was strongly encouraged. Over time some of these *ayllus* would unite for a common goal, if only temporarily. It is probable that the Inca empire began in just this way; although the *ayllus* remained strong, the central Inca government gained more power.

The concept of private ownership of land was foreign to the Amerindian way of thinking; land was shared in common by the community or state. Although each individual family was given a small plot of land to build a home and to grow a few plants, the larger portion of the community land was shared, the members of the *ayllu* working the land as a group. The idea of sharing was extended to mean caring for the weak and infirm of the community by the stronger, and by all men working each other's land at peak times of need. The land used by each family could not be bought or sold, and there was no prestige in its ownership. Land was viewed as a necessity, not as a commodity that could by traded.

INCA GOVERNMENT

The Inca called their empire *Tahuantinsuyu*, the "Land of the Four Quarters"; for purposes of administration it was divided into four sections. Each section was under the supervision of a member of the Imperial Council, usually an army commander, who was just below the Inca himself in power. The sections were further divided into provinces under the administration of a provincial governor, often a member of a conquered tribe whose loyalty had been won over. Finally, and most importantly, for they touched the daily lives of all Incas, were the **curacas** in charge of supervising and inspecting large subsections; minor inspectors supervised small *ayllus*. In order to keep the whole structure honest there were inspectors checking on all levels of government.

Above all others in the Inca government stood the person of the Inca, or Sapa Inca ("unique Inca"), the final authority on all matters. Part of his prestige rested on the purity of the Inca bloodline. From one of his sisters he would choose his main wife, or **coya**, and one of her sons would be designated as his heir. The Inca state was a **totalitarian** one, controlled by the Inca and his administrators. All aspects of the life of the Incas were dictated and supervised by the state, including what labour men and women should do, what clothes they should wear, where they should live, and even when and whom they should marry.

One of the most important of all Incas institutions was the **mita**, a tax on the labour of all men between the ages of sixteen and sixty. This took the form of an obligation to work for the Inca each year for a designated period. The form of work varied from soldiering to being a servant for the Inca nobility. Some were chosen for the important task of being a **chasqui**, a runner of messages on the roads of this far-flung empire. Others worked on the huge stone construction projects, or in the mines. Some men, however, could be exempted from *mita*, including skilled craftsmen and the all-important keepers of the *quipu*, or account-keepers.

The entire community would participate in the building of roads and bridges, terraces, forts, temples, and royal buildings. Everyone had to work and the crime of sloth was one of the more serious criminal acts against the state. The only exceptions to this were the skilled artisans who held the secrets of working with gold, silver, and copperwork. These secrets were passed from father to son.

Ten was a crucial age for young girls and boys. At this age some boys would be taken forever from the *ayllu* for service to a noble as a gift for the noble's loyalty, or for service to the Inca royal court. Those girls of par-

Fig. 4.5
These weary labourers are carrying their taxes, in the form of crops from government-owned fields, to government storehouses.

ticular beauty at age ten would also be taken from their *ayllus* to be **acllacuna**, legendary Inca "chosen women." They would be placed in "convents" around the empire for a four-year period, where they would maintain their purity while learning how to make rich *chicha* beer from fermented corn and how to weave beautiful cloths for the Inca.

After four years some *acllacuna* would be given to Inca nobles or soldiers as secondary wives, ranked below the *coya*, or principal wife. Others would live out a cloistered existence in the convent. Some, seen as the most rewarded of all, were chosen for a ceremonial sacrifice, often to be thrown down a well; they would enjoy an eternity of happiness in honour of this sacrifice.

The beautiful cloths and the *chicha* made at the convents played an important role in enhancing the power of the Inca. The *chicha* and the food prepared by the "chosen women" were served at festivals, events of heavy eating and drinking sometimes lasting twenty days, that helped keep the Inca subjects contented. Possession of the cloths was an essential part of the Inca ruler's prestige, and he used them as rewards for deserving subjects. All in all, it was considered a high honour to be one of the "chosen women," for the life of an *acllacuna* was a protected and luxurious one.

THE INCA CLASS SYSTEM

An Inca's station in life was set from the day he was born, and could not be altered. The Inca and his nobles lived a life of splendour well apart from the everyday working life of the common Inca man and woman. At the peak of the Inca empire the city of Cuzco, with an estimated population of 100 000, had beautiful stone palaces and public buildings for the Inca nobility. The Spanish accounts of the splendour of these buildings, filled with gold and silver, stunning vicuña wool tapestries, and sumptuous meals of fresh fish brought by runners from the sea, speak of a life of great luxury.

By contrast, as we have seen, the common Inca lived a life where hard work, simplicity, and conformity left little room for the imagination. Perhaps this is why the Incas never bothered to develop a written language. The commoners had security, however, and food was ample. The Inca diet consisted of meat from small guinea pigs, occasional llama meat, potatoes, corn, and some root vegetables. The potato was introduced to the world from Peru by the Spaniards and has proven to be a far greater gift to humanity than any other Inca treasure. Hunting was difficult without horses or good long-range weaponry, but some pigeons, rabbits, and deer supplemented the diet as extra sources of protein. The guinea pig thrived in the high altitude of the Andes; fed on household scraps, it provided most of the protein in the Inca diet. Guinea pigs were cooked by a heated stone placed in the stomach cavity after the insides had been removed.

Homes for the common people were one-room, windowless structures, which the Incas shared with their animals in cold weather. Moving homes was rare, and travel from place to place was not allowed. A humdrum existence was probably made more tolerable by the constant chewing of coca leaves, dulling the senses, and by the drinking of *chicha* beer.

SOCIAL ORGANIZATION

The Inca empire, despite its geographical extent and difficult terrain, was relatively stable and self-sufficient up to the time of the Spanish invasion. The people were fairly content, crime and rebellion were rare, and no Inca subject lacked the necessities of life.

What held the society together was that each Inca subject accepted his or her "place" in society. There was no **social mobility**; everyone stayed in the caste they were born to all their lives. While there was little or no room for imagination, inventiveness, and initiative in Inca life, there was security, and little true poverty, unemployment, or crime.

The empire worked through a system of regimentation, constant inspection, and continuous vigilance. Members of the *ayllu* were divided into squads of nine and an overseer. Five squads were supervised by a leader, and larger groupings of one hundred, five hundred, and a thousand were overseen by higher officials. Squad leaders supervised the work of all squad members and reported on the results of the work to government officials; these squad leaders distributed necessities such as wool, seed, and tools to their squad, according to need.

Most importantly for the stability of the empire, squad leaders had to report any crime or idleness by any subordinate immediately. Total conformity was expected by the Inca state, and any deviation was considered a crime. Even a one-day delay in reporting was considered criminal. Punishment was severe, often by whipping or stoning. For extremely serious crimes the entire *ayllu* was held equally responsible for the criminal act of one of its members and would be put to death with the criminal. The usual method was to be hung upside down until death. Prisons were unknown, but underground caverns filled with venomous snakes, jaguars, pumas, foxes, and vultures were occasionally used for punishment. Theft was almost never committed, and Inca homes were open all the time. The Incas were particularly disgusted by the Spaniards' thieving and looting.

RELIGION

On its simplest level, Inca religion continued age-old practices of nature worship. Each village left offerings at natural shrines. These included caves, large rock outgrowths, springs, and mountain tops. Plants and animals with mutations or which appeared strange in some way were also worshipped. The changing of the seasons was a time for great celebration.

On a second level the Incas worshipped the Inca and his royal family, who were seen as divine. The Inca was identified with the sun-god and was the centre of all Inca celebrations. Workers devoted themselves to him during their great construction projects, and religion played a large role in enabling the Inca successfully to mobilize so many men for these efforts.

On a third and higher level, Inca religion was a cult centring on the sun-god. The movements of the sun, moon, and other forces of nature were studied in detail. The moon, the wife of the sun and the mother of the Inca people, and the lightning, rainbow, and thunder gods were also worshipped. Inca conceptions of heaven and hell and the eternal soul were very complex, if at root somewhat similar to those of western religions, although their idea of hell was a very cold place where the soul would go hungry.

Temples to the sun were built everywhere as places for animal sacrifices. Human sacrifice was rare but was practised. A special group of the "chosen women," virgins of noble blood called "Virgins of the Sun," were sequestered in a convent to tend and guard the sacred fire used in the ceremony of the Festival of *Raymi*. This was a celebration of the summer solstice. These women had taken a vow of chastity. A "Virgin of the Sun" who was caught violating her vows was punished by being buried alive with her strangled lover.

For the Incas the most important of all religious occasions was the celebration of the Festival of *Raymi*. Pilgrims came to Cuzco from all over the empire. After a three-day fast, they would dress in their finest clothes and greet the rising of the sun on the day it reached its southernmost point. Beautifully decorated wool and feather canopies were held over the heads of Inca nobles, and when the sun came over the horizon it was greeted with music and shouting. A sacred fire was lit for the sun's journey by using a concave mirror to set fire to dry cotton.

The great temple of the sun, later sacked and destroyed by the Spaniards, was reputedly a marvel of engineering, wealth, and beauty. A large sun studded with precious stones was used for the altar, and the walls were covered with thin sheets of gold. The sun's rays were reflected from the walls, casting golden light throughout the temple. Embalmed corpses of dead Inca emperors, wrapped in beautiful cloth and looking very lifelike, sat on golden chairs on either side of the altar. The silver room of the moon was the resting place for the mummies of the Inca wives. Other gods had their own rooms. After the conquest the Spaniards tore down all this gold and silver and melted it down into bullion to be sent back to

Fig. 4.6
This sketch of the Temple of the Sun was drawn by a Spanish artist from descriptions given to him by those who had seen it before it was destroyed.

Spain. Only one-fifth of all the gold and silver, the share preserved for the King of Spain, remained in its original shape and form to recall Inca splendour.

INCA WEDDINGS

Individual preferences in courting and marriage were frowned upon by the Inca as a waste of effort, and as a process that inevitably left some men and women unattached. In a society such as theirs, with little left to waste or chance, such an unpredictable system was intolerable. Therefore, every year or so men of twenty-four years and women of eighteen years would be gathered together in the central plaza of each town, arbitrarily lined up across from each other, and united in matrimony by an Inca priest. In some cases lovers contrived to stand opposite each other. But unless this happened, there was no choice. All spouses had to come from the same community. After marriage a home was chosen for the newly-weds and placed as near to their work as possible. Polygamy was permitted only to the nobility, and incestuous marriage, that is, marriage to a close family member such as a sister, was restricted to the Inca and his heir.

INCA FARMING

Under the rule of the Incas the *ayllu* system became formalized, if slightly modified. A *tiered* system of land ownership and land division came into being. The concept of land ownership by the community became extended to mean that all land was owned by the state in trust for the people. A three-way division of the land then took place. Each individual *ayllu* was given enough land to feed its own members. As a result, hunger was unknown in the Inca empire, and this played no small role in maintaining stability. This was a paternalistic state in which the rulers provided for the well-being and the protection of their people. A second division of the land belonged to the gods; its yield went to the Inca priests for their support and for ceremonial use. The third division of land went to the Inca; its produce was used in the royal court and for the army.

All land was communally tended; the Inca's share was worked first, then the gods' share, and finally the *ayllu's* land. Heads of *ayllus* were allotted one *tupu*, approximately five hectares, for each male and half a *tupu* for each female. All healthy and able-bodied farmers were expected to share in the work, and foremen directed which plot should be cultivated at any particular time. Any farmer who tended his own plot before those of the aged and infirm was executed. Inca adjustors would survey land divisions every year and make adjustments based on changing needs.

Fish heads and guano, mostly from pelicans, were collected from the coast and used as fertilizer. A wooden plough in the form of a spade, with a crossbar for driving by the foot, was the main digging implement. By all surviving accounts the Incas worked the lands contentedly, singing songs about great Inca deeds and working to their rhythms. Everyone drank *chicha* beer and there was great co-operation all round.

Large herds of alpacas and llamas that were the property of the Inca and the sun had to be tended and periodically sheared. Some Inca farmers were excused from cultivation to become full-time shepherds, tending the flocks as the animals moved from place to place in order to find fresh pasture. All farmers would join in the shearing, and the wool would be stored centrally and distributed to families on the basis of need. The women wove the clothing for their family, a task done in the home and periodically inspected by the government for quality. When that was done the women then wove for the Inca.

The llama was the most important of the four camelids found in the Andes Mountains, and was the closest to a beast of burden in all of pre-Columbian America. This pack animal has a mass of about 200 kg and is the largest of the four camelid species found in the Americas. It can carry a load of about 60 kg, but it cannot pull heavy loads as an ox or horse can. When it is overloaded it will fall on its belly and refuse to move. The llama has a claw on its hoof that enables it to climb on rocks and ice. It can subsist on the sparse vegetation of the Andean range, and can go for weeks without water. Llama droppings are useful as fertilizer. The only other domesticated camelid was the smaller alpaca, an animal that produces a fine wool. The vicuña and guanaco are wild. In Inca

Fig. 4.7
The Andean alpaca, a domesticated wool-bearing animal, one of the four camelids found in the Andean region.

times they were rounded up once a year and sheared.

The Incas had the foresight to store food and wool in good years for years when the yield was poor, so there was never a shortage of either. Storehouses called **qollqas** were placed at points fifteen to twenty kilometres apart throughout the Inca realm, and were filled with wool, dehydrated food, shoes, and armaments for the use of military groups that might pass by. Detailed records were kept of what was in storage.

INCA ROADS AND BRIDGES

The Inca empire was so vast that it included climate regions varying from tropical to temperate. It comprised at least three diverse geographic regions, thought by the Spaniards to be uninhabitable, but nonetheless organized, administered, and farmed by the Incas. These were regions of huge mountain ranges with slopes rising in some places almost vertically to a height of nearly ten kilometres. These slopes were terraced and irrigated in order to produce food for the nearly six million subjects of the Inca.

The task of binding together this mountainous empire with a network of roads and bridges was a daunting one. The roads and bridges were engineering marvels, linking the entire empire with a transportation and communication network, and enabling the unity of the realm to be a functioning reality. Two parallel networks of roads linked the north and the south. One road ran through the mountains from northern Ecuador to Chile; the other was a coastal road from northern Peru to Chile. These roads covered tremendous distances. There were several roads running across the two main roads for east-west transport. For most of their extent the roads were narrow footpaths — all that was needed as the Inca did not have wheeled vehicles.

The road through the mountains had to cross ravines and deep chasms. Some ravines were filled in with enormous quantities of stone to form a road; others were crossed by suspension bridges made of heavy rope and tied to rocks on each side. These rope bridges would swing wildly, but were safe. The Spaniards were even able to walk their horses over them. The ropes, some as thick as a human body, were made from osier, a species of willow, interwoven with strong hemp. In some parts of the Andes this method of bridge-building is still used today.

The roads were used mainly by runners or couriers, called **chasquis**, to carry messages or small parcels such as fresh fruit or fish from one government outpost to another. Each town in the empire had to keep a group of *chasquis* ready for service at all times. A team of runners, working in short relays, could cover up to 400 km a day,

Fig. 4.8
The deepest ravines and the sheerest rocks were no match for Inca road engineers, who built bridges like this to ford any chasm. These bridges even took the weight of Spanish horses.

while running mostly uphill and at very high altitudes! Occasionally the Inca would travel, carried on an ornately decorated litter surrounded by thousands of warriors, nobles, pages, and other attendants.

ARCHITECTURE

The stonework of Inca buildings was fitted together without mortar, and was so ex-

Fig. 4.9
The giant stone walls of Sacsayhuaman illustrate the phenomenal Inca stonework. The stones are so closely fitted together that a knife blade cannot penetrate between them. These walls have withstood several earthquakes in the past centuries, and remain standing even to this day.

pertly hewn that even a sharp blade could not pierce the cracks between the stones. The stones were apparently cut into shape by hard reeds shaped into saws. These reeds grew abundantly all over the empire. The stonework was so well built that much of it survived the forces of nature, including earthquakes, over many centuries. The surfaces of the stones were smoothed.

Magnificent Inca ruins are to be found in many parts of the former empire; some of these ruins have been built on the ruins of even more ancient pre- Inca buildings. The fortress of **Sacsayhuaman**, one of the most important of all Inca remains, was built on a hillside north of Cuzco. Its three towers were to protect the city. The towers were themselves protected by three enormous zigzagged walls, with stones so large that many observers could not believe the fort was built by humans. The stones were exceptionally smooth and perfectly cut to fit in an interlocking pattern, so well crafted that the Spaniards tore much of the walls apart to use these beautiful stones for their buildings in Cuzco. It is said the walls of the fortress took 30 years to build by an army of over 20 000 men.

Undoubtedly the most famous of all Inca ruins is at **Machu Picchu**, thought to be one of three fortresses built to guard the mountain passes to Cuzco. Today it attracts the archaeologist and tourist alike by its beauty and mystery. First shown to an American explorer named Hiram Bingham by a local Amerindian guide in 1911, Machu Picchu is

Fig. 4.10
Machu Picchu, now deserted, was once a stronghold of the Incas, although its actual purpose is unclear. It may have been a convent as well as a fortress. Its beauty testifies to the great skills of Inca stonemasons.

orchids grow, and its obvious impregnability to attack, still stimulate the senses and the imagination.

While much Inca architecture was colossal in size, building methods were very simple. Nails were not used; ceilings were supported by beams, and roofs were made from thatch up to two metres thick, which constantly needed repair . Doors and windows were narrow, insides of buildings were semi-lit and dank. Hallways were unknown, and one room just seemed to open on another.

SCIENCE, MEDICINE, AND TECHNOLOGY

In most areas of abstract knowledge the Inca were inferior to the Classic Period Maya. Although they had made a study of the sun, moon, and stars, they failed to adapt this knowledge to a satisfactory calendar. The Inca calendar was based on the erratic lunar month, with an extra month inserted periodically by the Inca when planting and harvesting fell out of sequence with calendar dates.

The exception to Inca inferiority in science and technology was in the field of medicine, especially surgery. Inca surgeons were able to carry out relatively sophisticated medical treatments such as amputating limbs and setting fractures. They knew the use of bandages, tourniquets, and forceps. Amazingly, skeletal remains show successful healings from **trepanning**, the removal of a section of the skull with drills, saws, and chisels. This was done to relieve pain and pressure from a wound to the head

one of the best preserved of all Inca ruins, unsullied by Spanish conquerors. The abandoned town at the site is preserved in excellent condition, and historians debate over what the actual function of Machu Picchu was. There is a wide variety of hypotheses about its use, from a convent for the "Virgins of the Sun" to a military outpost, to a retreat for the Inca nobility, and even to the last refuge of the Incas from the Spanish. In any case, its spectacular beauty, surrounded by mountains where lilies and suffered in battle. The brain often had to be kept in the skull during and after the operation by the use of a shell as a stopper. The Incas also discovered the use of *quinine*, from evergreen bark, and used it as a drug to relieve the pain of operations; they used resin from the balsam trees to stop bleeding, speed healing, and expel parasitic worms.

Although the Incas made few advances in most areas of science and technology, they were clever adaptors of the science and technology of the people they conquered and assimilated.

QUIPUS

Knotted multi-coloured strings called **quipus** were used for keeping Inca accounts and records. Since the Incas had no written language and lacked even a pictographic or hieroglyphic form of writing, surviving *quipus*, limited as they are to numerical data, remain the only "written" record they left behind. Yet, because there are no longer any Inca keepers of the *quipus*, or "rememberers" of the meaning of the knots, the information that surviving *quipus* contain has been lost to history.

Births and deaths, payments to workers, important dates, storage statistics for food and wool, and other similar kinds of data were recorded on a *quipu* by tying knots in certain patterns on a main or stem cord approximately 60 to 70 cm in length. Thus no two *quipus* were ever exactly alike. The number, relative placement, thickness, and colour of the knots had significance in determining what they represented, and each town had keepers who memorized the meaning of the *quipu* knots. The *quipu*

knots record the information; the actual totalling up was probably done with stones and pebbles or special counting trays, a method that is still used in parts of the Andes today. The Incas used the decimal system, and had developed the concept of zero. This important mathematical insight only occurred three times in history: during the Mayan civilization; in India, from where it came to Arabia and the West; and in the Inca civilization.

Dates would be recorded simply as the numbered day or year, but to the keeper of the *quipu* it would have a symbolism that would remind him of an important event that took place at that time. Each keeper would store hundreds of such knotted strings, kept coiled in jars. These "rememberers" would explain to each other the significance of the knots. Important history was thus passed from generation to generation. But after the Spanish conquest, when the last person who could read the *quipu* died, knowledge of the history was lost. The Spaniards burned the vast majority of *quipus* in the belief that they represented non-Christian beliefs and practices. Today experts cannot tell if surviving *quipus* represent food, gold, warriors, taxes, llamas, or for that matter, anything else.

PART THREE: THE SPANISH CONQUEST

THE ARRIVAL OF THE SPANIARDS

The great Inca leader Huayna Capac loved the pleasant climate in the north of the Inca

Fig. 4.11

The Inca quipu-keeper on the right makes a financial report to a high official.

empire. After his successful expansion of the empire into present-day Colombia, he built the city of Quito and settled there. In the spring of 1528 disturbing reports reached his palace that ships had arrived off the coast containing strange-looking men never before seen in the realm. A second disturbing event soon followed. An epidemic of what is thought to have been smallpox struck the empire, and killed among others Huayna Capac, his eldest son and heir, and a good part of the royal government. It is estimated that more than 200 000 Amerindians died as the plague spread through every region. It devastated and demoralized the Amerindians when they were about to face their greatest threat, that of the Spanish invasion.

The Spanish conquest of Peru started with events in Panama in 1522, where the Spanish conquistadore Balboa had crossed the mountainous Panamanian isthmus on a historic march to the Pacific Ocean. He and his men were among the first Europeans to see the Pacific, which he claimed in the name of the Spanish sovereign. Here local Amerindians told Balboa and his men about long-necked sheep and, more importantly, great stores of gold to be found further south. Balboa was never to find this gold, as he was charged with treason by his jealous rival, the governor of Panama, and beheaded.

A forty-year-old former Spanish swineherd, Francisco Pizarro, had accompanied Balboa on the march across the mountains of Panama to the Pacific. Pizarro, who was born in Spain sometime in the 1470s, had never learned how to write his name, and one legend about his origins has him wet-nursed by a sow. But despite these humble beginnings he had risen to prestige among the soldiers by heroic actions in numerous expeditions, and before his death he became one of the wealthiest men in the Spanish empire. Along with Cortés, he is remembered as one of the two greatest conquistadores.

In league with two other plotters, one of them the illiterate and equally treacherous Diego de Almagro, Pizarro formed a partnership with the goal of conquering the fabled empire. After collecting some 20 000 pesos from Spanish investors in Panama, he and a small band of less than 100 men set out on an expedition in 1524.

Fig. 4.12
Francisco Pizarro, conqueror of the Inca empire

Landing several thousand kilometres north of the actual location of the Inca empire, the men were besieged by insects and torrential rains. They found only a few poisonous wild berries and some shellfish to eat, and virtually all suffered from malnutrition. Twenty of his men starved to death. This original attempt at entering the Inca empire was a failure, and Pizarro and his surviving men had to return to Panama in a greatly weakened condition. Yet because a small amount of gold articles had been found among the local Amerindians, Pizarro was determined to launch another expedition.

Pizarro was forced to turn back from a second attempt in 1528. By now these failures had discredited him and held him up to ridicule in the eyes of his investors, among whom were the governor and church leaders in Panama. Investments for a third voyage were not forthcoming. Pizarro tried one last source. In 1528 he sailed for Spain, where he presented gold and silver jewelry, llamas, and beautiful tapestries made from vicuña wool to King Charles I.

Pizarro's timing was fortunate, for Cortés had only recently brought back gold from Mexico, and so the optimistic King named Pizarro governor of Peru for life, with a large salary. (This elevation of Pizarro over Almagro was later to divide the partners in a way that eventually led to both their deaths.) Pizarro then visited his birthplace, where he recruited his four brothers for his enterprise. After his return to Panama, he sailed in late 1530 for the west coast of South America, this time with nearly 180 men and 27 horses.

After a voyage of two weeks he decided to land on the Ecuador coast; from there he and his men moved inland. He raided a town, obtaining gold and silver, which he sent back to Panama to be used to recruit more soldiers. As Pizarro was suffering some ill health, he settled for a spell on the coast. After he recovered, he and his men crossed the jungle into the north of Peru, and stopped at the Inca fortress at Tumbez. Here he learned of divisions within the empire, and remembering Cortés' success in dividing the Mexican Amerindians, he made a mental note of this for future use. Hernando de Soto, later to be remembered as the European discoverer of the Mississippi River, reinforced him at Tumbez with fresh soldiers, and they prepared to march into the main stronghold of the Inca empire.

While Pizarro's luck held, the luck of the Inca was all bad. With the Inca Huayna Capac dead from smallpox, his empire was embroiled in a war over the inheritance of the realm. Foolishly, this last great Inca had died without specifying a single heir, dividing the empire between two of his sons. This led to a struggle between them; the late Inca's advisors chose Huascar, the son of the Inca's *coya*. The generals and common people preferred another son, Atahualpa, rumoured to have been Huayna Capac's favourite. Huascar lost in this power struggle and became a captive of Atahualpa, later to be murdered by him. Pizarro had arrived at a rare point in the history of the empire when there was a lack of unity and a civil war between two royal heirs. He was able as a result to enlist the aid of Amerindian auxiliary soldiers, which he could not have done at a time of Inca unity.

THE CAPTURE OF THE INCA

Pizarro, with 62 soldiers dragging their horses, and 106 foot soldiers, climbed almost on all fours over a steep mountain barrier. After a difficult journey of nearly two months they reached the Inca city of Cajamarca, only to find it deserted. The Inca residents were all encamped near the city with nearly 30 000 Inca troops. Also present was the Inca, Atahualpa. De Soto and 35 mounted soldiers, in an attempt to intimidate the Amerindians, rode hard into the camp (horses had never before been seen by the Inca) and stopped just short of the Inca. Atahualpa, however, sat completely still and silent. At length his natural curiosity and an invitation by Pizarro promising to meet him "as a friend and brother" convinced him to meet with Pizarro the next day.

De Soto's report of the huge number of Inca warriors instilled fear among the Spanish soldiers. Pizarro, realizing he needed to act boldly, and with the example of Cortés' successful seizure of Moctezuma in mind, resolved that a capture of the Inca was his only hope. In preparation for the Inca's visit — a preparation that included much desperate prayer — all horsemen and soldiers were placed in hiding.

As the Inca was carried into the city, borne by nobles on a golden throne placed on a litter, and accompanied by thousands of soldiers, no Spaniard was in sight. At this point the Spanish priest Valverde appeared with a crucifix and a Bible to proclaim the **requerimiento** (requirement), a call for the Inca to recognize the authority of King and Pope. The punishment for non-recognition was slavery and seizure of all property, even wives. Through a rough translation the Inca understood he was being required to surrender and, outraged, threw the Bible that had been given to him to the ground. This book, which he thought an unimpressive god, was to him merely a covered group of very thin, cut leaves. Greatly angered, Valverde now shouted "Attack at once, I absolve you."

Spanish soldiers were signalled by bugle to open fire, and men on horseback, in full

Fig. 4.13
This eighteenth century Flemish engraving shows Atahualpa on his litter in the centre as he and the unarmed Inca army are savagely attacked by the Spaniards. Thousands of Incas were killed, and Atahualpa was taken prisoner.

battle cry, waded into the defenceless Incas. Some Incas courageously grabbed the horses' legs to try to keep them away from the Inca ruler. As litter bearers were cut down, their limbs mercilessly sliced off, others took their place, until the Inca's litter could no longer be held aloft. The sound of cannon panicked the Incas; nearly seven thousand of them were hunted down and slain mercilessly. The Inca himself was taken prisoner. All this took place without even the serious wounding of a single Spanish soldier.

The Inca army stood by helplessly while their leader was held prisoner. Atahualpa was treated with great deference, and was allowed to keep his servants. He even learned to play chess with his captors. When he realized the Spaniards had a great love for gold he promised that for his release he would fill up the room, said to have been about five by six metres, in which he was held captive, with gold from the empire. A written agreement was signed, and over the next two months Incas from all corners of the realm brought gold jewelry and other forms of beautiful Inca goldwork to fill the room.

Outside the room a boiling vat worked day and night to melt all this priceless art into gold bars to be shared out among the soldiers. Only the King's fifth was preserved in its original artistic form, and this is all that is left today of the beautiful Inca goldwork. Each soldier was now worth about 40 kg of gold, a fortune in those days. Yet even with all of this gold the soldiers were anxious for more, as unfounded rumours circulated that much more gold was secreted by Inca priests in the native temples. Under pressure from his men Pizarro turned treacherous. He broke his side of the bargain with Atahualpa and charged him, without evidence, with inspiring a revolt. After a mockery of a trial the Inca was executed.

THE FALL OF THE EMPIRE

Without the semi-divine figure of the Inca at its head, the empire now began to descend into **anarchy**, and some recently conquered territories proclaimed their independence. Pizarro, who had effectively ruled the empire through the hostage Inca, recognized his error in destroying Atahualpa. A puppet Inca under his control was placed on the throne. He then set out to seize control of the empire. In 1533 Pizarro and his men captured Cuzco and tortured many of its population. The Spaniards looted temples and palaces, and violated the women of the town. Even Cuzco's tombs were destroyed in the search for more gold. Any illusions the Incas had had that the Spaniards marked the return of the creator-god Viracocha were now shattered.

From this year onwards the rest of the Inca empire was brought under Spanish control. Pizarro established a capital at Lima, on the coast, to symbolize his rule. He was now in dispute however, with his former partner, Almagro, over the control of Cuzco, and also with his puppet Inca, Manco, who was rebelling against him.

Manco, having realized the Spaniards were enslaving his people, raided Spanish outposts all over the empire. He placed Cuzco under a year-long siege and was only defeated when Pizarro's partner Almagro and his army returned from an unsuccessful expedition to Chile. Pizarro, now reinforced, and further helped because many of Manco's soldiers had to return to their homes to sow seed for the next year's crop, was finally able to disperse the Inca forces besieging the city.

Almagro then captured Cuzco, claimed it for his share of the partnership, and imprisoned two of Pizarro's brothers. A civil war broke out among the Spaniards; eventually Almagro was captured by Pizarro supporters, tried, convicted, condemned to death, and garrotted (strangled). Pizarro now was free to crush the last Inca resistance. In time Pizarro himself was venge-

Fig. 4.14

The execution of the last Inca Tupa Amaru by the Spaniards in 1572. In this century some Latin American revolutionary groups have taken this Inca's name as their own and have called themselves the Tupamaros.

fully murdered in Lima by the *mestizo* son of Almagro, but not before stabbing three of his assassins in the throat.

Manco continued his resistance by setting up a capital at the jungle site of Vilcabamba, far from Spanish-occupied Cuzco, where he executed Pizarro's peace emissaries. In retaliation Pizarro had Manco's sister-wife tied naked to a tree and stabbed to death. Manco held out for nine years. He was joined by seven supporters of Almagro, including the murderers of

Pizarro, who taught him Spanish and the use of swords and guns. Finally he was stabbed in the back by one of these murderers.

Vilcabamba continued its resistance by guerilla attacks from the jungle against Spanish settlements until the Spaniards entered this last Inca stronghold in 1572. The last Inca, the legendary Tupa Amaru, escaped into the jungle where he and his pregnant wife were eventually captured and beheaded. Thus ended the Inca reign.

REASONS FOR THE DEFEAT OF THE INCAS

Why did this vast, seemingly secure and stable empire fall relatively quickly and easily to Pizarro and his small band of men? Many theories have been proposed, and perhaps there is no single explanation. Isolated from the rest of the world, lacking knowledge of the fate of the Aztecs, and without understanding the military superiority of soldiers on horseback with gunpowder, the Inca had no way of gauging the full danger posed by the arrival of the Spaniards. In fact, by the sixteenth century the Incas were convinced they had conquered most of the civilized world. Also, like the Aztecs, they were further weakened by their belief in the ancient legend that the Spaniards represented the creator-god Viracocha and were a fulfillment of his promise to return someday.

Diseases brought by the Spaniards, against which the native populations had little immunity, also played a part in the Inca downfall. To Amerindians who had no experience with epidemics, the Spaniards seemed to have some sort of divine dispensation from these illnesses. Indian religions recognized that gods often acted in anger against humans, and the Inca therefore concluded that the gods favoured the Spaniards. In addition to immunity from disease, the Spaniards seemed to be successful no matter how small their numbers or how brutal their actions. Inca authority, always based on religious authority, crumbled everywhere and with it Inca institutions collapsed.

The death of the Inca Hauyna Capac and other leaders from the smallpox epidemic severely weakened the empire, leaving the people with no clear successor to the dead Inca. The struggle for succession resulted in civil war, shaking the unity of the empire on the eve of the Spanish invasion. With no clear central authority, the highly conformist and dependent Inca population was bereft of leadership at a crucial time. Imaginative and individual leadership from anyone but the Inca was simply unthinkable.

The victor in the succession struggle, Atahualpa, accustomed to commanding armies of thousands, underestimated the danger from the small number of Spaniards. Reports that the Spaniard's horses were tied up at night led him to believe the animals were useless after dusk. At several points along the Spanish march inland, along narrow ledges high above deep ravines or in tight mountain passes, the advance could have been stopped by a small group of Inca soldiers. Later, attempting to trap the Spaniards, Atahualpa himself was trapped and ultimately destroyed. This contrasts with Pizarro's brilliant stroke of destroying the basis of Inca unity in a single blow by his capture of the Inca.

Any assessment of Pizarro must rank him among the great conquerors of history. Over a period of eighteen years he overcame countless geographical obstacles. The empire he conquered was even larger than that conquered by Cortés. Pizarro's strengths were his courage and persistence. But he lacked the vision of Cortés, and did not inspire the loyalty of his men in the same way the conqueror of the Aztecs did, possibly because he was illiterate and lacked a strong religious conviction, Nor was he able to reconcile the conquerors with the conquered in the same way Cortés eventually did. Although both men sought money and power and were prepared to act cruelly and brutally to obtain them, at least the conqueror of Mexico could argue that his conquest put an end to a barbaric religion based on human sacrifice.

In the century following, the Amerindians of the former Inca empire were almost totally wiped out. The population is estimated to have fallen from five or six million at the time of the Spanish arrival to some 600 000 by 1620, a decline of nearly ninety per cent. The immigration of 20 000 Spaniards in the sixteenth century brought new diseases to this previously isolated people: especially measles, the common cold, influenza, mumps, diphtheria, typhus, and particularly smallpox. Diseases that were merely bothersome to the European were deadly to the Amerindian.

The Spaniards came to believe they had a right to enslave Amerindians and to exploit their labour. This contributed to the popu-

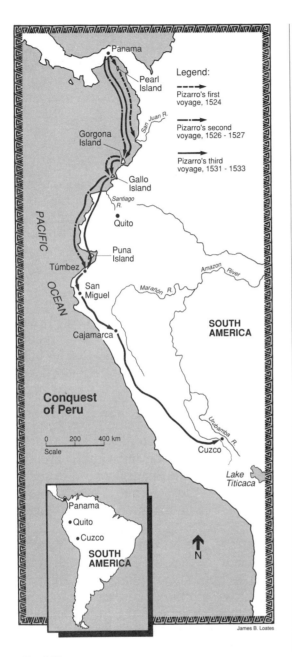

Fig. 4.15
The conquest of Peru

lation decline. Thousands died from pneumonia and malnutrition after being conscripted to work all day in the humid and foul air of the silver mines. Many Amerindians were murdered, despite the exhortations of Christian missionaries and others to treat the natives with decency. Finally, the loss of dignity, self-worth, and sense of pride cannot be underestimated as a cause of Amerindian population decline. Suicide was rampant in the post-conquest period, as were abortion and infanticide.

From this point onwards the Amerindians would be subject to the laws of the conqueror with the gun and the horse. The end of the Inca empire was the end of the last great pre-Columbian civilization.

A CHRONOLOGY OF THE INCA EMPIRE FROM THE 12TH CENTURY TO 1572

ca. late 12th Century	Manco Capac, semi-mythical son of the sun, founds Inca dynasty and becomes first Inca
1438-1471	Pachacuti, ninth Inca and son of Viracocha, begins era of great Inca conquests. Empire expands beyond Cuzco to become Tahuantinsuyu, Four Quarters of the World
ca. 1470s	Francisco Pizarro is born in Spain
1471-1493	Inca lands expand to include a great domain under Tupa Inca, son of Pachacuti, one of

	the great conquerors of history
1493-1527	Empire expands to its fullest extent under Huayna Capac, son of Tupa Inca and last great Inca conqueror
1511	Pizarro accompanies Balboa as Spaniards discover Pacific Ocean; hears tales of great empire to the south
1524	Pizarro's first expedition to Inca territory ends in failure
1527	Pizarro's second expedition gets as far as Tumbez, confirms Inca wealth
	Death of Huayna Capac from smallpox; struggle for succession between two of his sons, Huascar and Atahualpa
1528	Incas learn of the presence of strange men in the empire; smallpox brought by the Spaniards kills thousands of Amerindians including the Inca
1529	King Charles I of Spain names Pizarro governor of Peru
1530	Pizarro returns to Panama; signs contract with Almagro and third partner
1532	Pizarro and his expedition reach northern Peru with 168 men, 62 horses, and 2 cannon; Atahualpa is captured at Cajamarca; Huascar is killed
March 1533	Atahualpa bargains with Pizarro for his freedom; orders gold from all over the empire brought to Pizarro
July 1533	Gold is melted down and distributed to soldiers; Atahualpa is killed when Pizarro does not keep bargain
November 1533	Siege of Cuzco; Cuzco sacked by Spaniards
December 1533	Manco Inca is crowned new Inca by Spaniards
1535	Manco Inca rebels; Inca siege of Cuzco
April 1537	Almagro returns from Chile; relieves siege of Cuzco; demands Cuzco as his share of empire from Pizarro; war among Spaniards breaks out
April 1538	Pizarro defeats Almagro; Almagro is executed
1539	Last Inca stronghold at Vilcabamba is captured by Spaniards
July 1541	Pizarro assassinated in Lima
1541	Murderers of Pizarro

are given protection by Manco Inca; Manco murdered by Spaniards

1541-1572   Consolidation of Spanish conquest continues as Inca empire crumbles; last Inca, Tupa Amaru, is captured in 1572 and executed: massive decline in Amerindian population due to introduction of new diseases

HIGHLIGHTS

1. The Inca empire controlled the Andean region for more than a century until the Spanish invasion of the 1520s. The Incas had no written language; what we know about them comes largely from Spanish chroniclers and from artifacts.
2. Although the Incas are the best known of all Andean civilizations, many pre-Inca cultures existed such as the Chavin, Nazca, Moche, Chimú, and Tiahuanaco.
3. After the collapse of the Tiahuanaco culture the Andean peoples reverted from urban civilization to a more simple farming culture. Sometime in the twelfth century one of the feuding tribes emerged as dominant over the others, possibly because of their ability to organize and to adapt the best of others' ideas. This tribe was the Incas.
4. Under the leadership of the great Inca Pachacuti the Inca empire began to expand in the fifteenth century, and the empire reached its fullest extent in the early sixteenth century.
5. The Inca's fighting methods were simple, but they had a talent for organization and an excellent road network. Many tribes surrendered to them rather than fight.
6. The conquest of the empire was consolidated by *mitima*, the resettlement of potential rebels in loyal regions, and by indoctrination of the royal family of the conquered tribe.
7. The key institution of Inca life was the *ayllu*, an extended kin group. Land was divided into three sections: one for the *ayllu*, a second for the gods, and a third for the Inca. Land could not be bought or sold; it was worked by the *allyu*. The *ayllu* cared for its weak, needy, and aged.
8. All men between sixteen and sixty owed service to the Inca in the form of farming or other duties to support the royal court. The Inca class system was very rigid with little room for, or expectation of, social mobility.
9. The Inca nobility lived a life of splendour and luxury surrounded by goldwork and exquisite tapestries. By contrast the common Inca lived a simple life.
10. The potato was introduced to the world by the Andean people.
11. There were three levels of Inca religion: ancient worship of objects of nature; worship of the Inca and his royal family; and worship of heavenly bodies, especially the sun. A great temple to the sun at Cuzco, filled with magnificent goldwork, was sacked by the Spaniards.

12. Inca mass weddings would be held annually; boys of twenty-four were arbitrarily married to girls of eighteen.

13. The entire empire was served by a network of roads and rope bridges, some over deep chasms or nearly vertical mountains. This network was an important factor in the unity of the empire.

14. Inca stonework was exceptional: colossal boulders fitted together so perfectly that a fine blade could not penetrate the cracks. Stone structures like Sacsayhuaman and Machu Picchu still amaze modern observers with their massive and beautiful stone walls.

15. One important area of Inca achievement was in surgery, especially trepanning — relieving pressure on the brain by drilling a hole in it.

16. Although the Incas had no written language they were able to keep detailed records of all figures on knotted cords called *quipus*. Special readers of these *quipus* were able to interpret the meaning of the knots by their colour, thickness, and placement. The ability to read this information has been lost.

17. In 1528, strange white visitors were seen, followed by an outbreak of a smallpox epidemic. A victim of the epidemic was the Inca, who died without designating an heir. A struggle for succession divided the empire on the eve of the Spanish invasion.

18. Overcoming tremendous obstacles, Pizarro and his men invaded the Inca empire and took the Inca hostage. After bargaining for his freedom with the gold of the empire, the Inca was executed by Pizarro, who appointed a puppet Inca to replace him.

19. Following the Spanish sack of Cuzco, Pizarro quarrelled with his partner Almagro, who had claimed the riches of Cuzco for his share of Peru. Eventually Almagro was captured and executed, but in revenge Almagro supporters assassinated Pizarro.

20. Inca resistance continued under Manco Inca until he was murdered by Almagro supporters, to whom he had given protection. The last Inca stronghold of Vilcabamba was captured and the last Inca, Tupa Amaru, was executed in 1572.

21. The reasons for the Inca downfall have long been debated; they include the Inca underestimation of the Spanish threat, the lack of unity in the empire, and the introduction of new diseases that killed Amerindians in large numbers.

22. In the century following the Spanish arrival the Inca population declined by ninety per cent. While some of this was due to murder and exploitation by the Spaniards, most died from successive waves of new diseases such as measles and influenza.

TERMS TO UNDERSTAND

Write a one-sentence explanation of each of the following terms. Write a sentence using each term.

adobe
acllacuna
anarchy
ayllu

chasquis
coya
curacas
mestizo
middens
mita
mitima
paternalism
qollqas
quipus
requerimiento
sierra
social mobility
totalitarian
trepanning

DEVELOPING CRITICAL THINKING ABOUT CONCEPTS IN THE SOCIAL SCIENCES

1. *BASIC CHARACTERISTICS OF A CIVILIZATION*: Draw up a chart comparing the basic characteristics of Inca civilization as covered in this chapter (e.g. government, warfare, class system, religion, architecture, etc) with another ancient civilization, or with our civilization. Draw conclusions about how social, economic, and political forms of a society reinforce its basic values.
2. *MALE AND FEMALE ROLES AND REALITIES*: Assess the role of men and women in Inca society as a reflection of economic and military roles. Compare and contrast this with another ancient civilization or with our society.
3. *FORMS OF GOVERNMENT*: How does the Inca form of governing compare to other ancient societies; to other totalitarian societies of the twentieth century? Compare totalitarian government with democracy. Could the Inca empire have functioned democratically? Explain.
4. *THE IMPACT OF RELIGIOUS BELIEFS*: What was the impact of the Inca religious beliefs on Inca daily life? How did these beliefs affect the history of the empire? Compare this with another ancient society or with our society today.
5. *CASTE SYSTEMS*: Compare the Inca caste system with that of the Aztecs. Which was more rigid? Which better served the needs of its empire? Do we have a class system? Explain.
6. *MULTIPLE CAUSATION*: List the causes for the defeat of the Inca empire and then prioritize them in order of importance. Be prepared to defend your order to your classmates.
7. *MARITAL CUSTOMS*: Compare the Inca marital customs with marital customs from other societies. Assess how well these customs served the needs of their society. What are some of our marital customs? Do they serve the needs of our society well? What are their strengths and weaknesses?

RELATED TOPICS FOR RESEARCH AND PRESENTATION

Any of the pre-Inca civilizations: Chavín, Nazca, Moche, Chimú, Tuahuanaco
Machu Picchu
Sacsayhuaman
The mystery of the Nazca lines
Iberia in the sixteenth century

Inca medicine
Amerindians of the Andean region today

FOR ADDITIONAL READING AND RESEARCH

MAGAZINE AND JOURNAL ARTICLES

"Chan Chan, Peru's Ancient City of Kings," Michael Moseley and Carol J. Mackey, *National Geographic*, March 1973.

"Discovering the New World's Richest Unlooted Tomb," W. Alva, *National Geographic*, October, 1988.

"The Five Worlds of Peru," Kenneth F. Weaver, *National Geographic*, February 1964.

"Inca Child," P. Tierney, *Omni Magazine*, August 1984.

"A King Tut for the New World," *U. S. News & World Report*, September 26, 1988.

"The Lady of the Lines," L. Gomez, *Life Magazine*, November 1984.

"Long Before the Inca," R. L. Burger, *Natural History*, February, 1989.

"The Lost Empire of the Incas," Loren McIntyre, *National Geographic*, December 1973.

"Machu Picchu: Lost City of the Incas," J. F. Diggs, *U. S. News and World Report*, January 25, 1982.

"Mausoleum Brings Moche Culture to Life," *Science News*, September 17, 1988.

"Move Over King Tut," (Moche Tomb), M. Clark, *Newsweek*, September 26, 1988.

"Mystery of the Ancient Nazca Lines," Loren McIntyre, *National Geographic*, May 1975.

"Peru's Rites of Renewal," *Americas*, May/June, 1988.

"Raiders of the Lost City," A. M. Bingham, *American Heritage Magazine*, July/August, 1987.

"The Secrets of a Moche Lord," D. Thompson, *Time*, September 26, 1988.

"A Sister City at Machu Picchu," *Newsweek Magazine*, July 4, 1983.

"Surprise Discovery at Machu Picchu," S. Hammer, *Science Digest*, March 1984.

"Titicaca, Abode of the Sun," Harvey Arden, *National Geographic*, March 1982.

"Unravelling the Mystery of the Warrior Priest," C. B. Dennan, *National Geographic*, October, 1988.

"Unresolved Mysteries of the Incas," R. Schiller, *Readers Digest*, June 1982.

BOOKS

Anton, Ferdinand, *Ancient Peruvian Textiles*. Thames & Hudson, London, 1987.

Bennett, William C. and Junius B. Bird, *Andean Culture History*. Natural History Press, Garden City, New York, 1964.

Conrad, W. Conrad, and Arthur A. Demarest, *Religion and Empire, The Dynamics of Aztec and Inca Expansionism*. Cambridge University Press, 1984.

Emmerich, André, *Sweat of the Sun and Tears of the Moon*. Hacker Art Books, New York, 1977.

Hadingham Evan, *Lines to the Mountain Gods: Nazca and the Mysteries of Peru*. Random House, New York, 1987.

von Hagen, Victor W., *Realm of the Incas*. Mentor Books, New York, 1961.

Hemming, John, *The Conquest of the Incas*. Macmillan, London, 1970.

———, *Machu Picchu*. Newsweek Book Division, New York, 1981.

———, *Monuments of the Incas*. Little, Brown, Boston, 1982.

Keating, Richard W., *Peruvian Prehistory: An Overview of Pre-Inca and Inca Society*. Cambridge University Press, New York 1988.

Kubler, George, *The Art and Architecture of Ancient America: The Mexican, Maya, and Andean Peoples*. Penguin Books, Baltimore, 1962.

Jennings, Jesse D., *Ancient South Americans*. W. H. Freeman, San Francisco, 1983.

Lanning, Edward P., *Peru Before the Incas*. Prentice-Hall, Englewood Cliffs, New Jersey, 1967.

Mason, J. Alden, *The Ancient Civilizations of Peru*. Harmondsworth, London, 1957.

McIntyre, Loren, *The Incredible Incas and Their Timeless Land*. National Geographic Society, Washington D. C., 1975.

Morrison T., *Pathways to the Gods*. Harper and Row, London, 1978.

Moseley, Michael E., and Kent Day, eds., *Chan Chan: Andean Desert City*. University of New Mexico Press, Albuquerque, New Mexico, 1982.

Prescott, William H., *History of the Conquest of Peru*. Random House, New York.

Soustelle, Jacques, *The Route of the Incas*. Viking Press, New York, 1977.

Picture Credits

Chapter 1
14: Illustrations by Sue Gauthier
21, 23: D. Donne Bryant Stock Photography.

Chapter 2
30: MTLB. 32: Frederick Catherwood. 35: After Maudsley/MTLB. 37: Frederick Catherwood/MTLB. 38; The Bettmann Archive. 42: From *An Album of Maya Architecture*, by Tatiana Prouskouriakoff. New edition copyright © 1963 by the University of Oklahoma Press. 44: From the Dresden Codex. 47: MTLB. 48: Peabody Museum of Archaeology and Ethnology. 51: Filmteam/D. Donne Bryant Stock Photography. 52: All Rights Reserved — The Metropolitan Museum of Art. 55: From *An Album of Maya Architecture*, by Tatiana Prouskouriakoff. New edition copyright © 1963 by the University of Oklahoma Press. 58: Courtesy TV Ontario.

Chapter 3
68: Library of Congress/MTLB. 69, 70: MTLB. 74: Neg. No. 326597. Courtesy Department Library Services, American Museum of Natural History. 75: MTLB. 76: From the Florentine Codex/MTLB. 79: From the Mendoza Codex/MTLB. 81: MTLB. 83: Museum fur Völkerkunde, Vienna. 86: The Bettmann Archive. 89: The Bodleian Library, Oxford/MTLB. 94, 99: From Sahagun, *Historia de las Cosas de Neuva Espana*/MTLB. 95, 97: MTLB.

Chapter 4
111: Miguel/The Image Bank Canada. 114: Carolyn Kerson/D. Donne Bryant Stock Photography. 117, 121: Guaman Poma de Ayala/MTLB. 124: Laurent Saint-Cricq, *Voyage à Travers l'Amerique du Sud*, Paris, 1868/MTLB. 126: MTLB. 127: Guaman Poma de Ayala/MTLB. 128 (large photo): Bill Parsons/D. Donne Bryant Photography. 128 (inset): Harold M. Lambert/Miller Comstock. 129: Patrick Knight/Canapress Photo Service. 131, 132: The Bettmann Archive. 134: MTLB. 136: Guaman Poma de Ayala/MTLB.